I0412964

Tracing My Roots in Guanajuato, León, and Silao's Haciendas and Ranchos

(*1734–1945*)

Tracing My Roots in Guanajuato, León, and Silao's Haciendas and Ranchos (*1734–1945*)

MAURICIO JAVIER GONZÁLEZ

Copyright © 2017 by Mauricio Javier González.

Book cover image: Andrés González and Tomasa Díaz, Silao, Guanajuato, early 1930s

Library of Congress Control Number:		2017901653
ISBN:	Hardcover	978-1-5065-1887-9
	Softcover	978-1-5065-1886-2
	eBook	978-1-5065-1885-5

All rights reserved. No part of this book may be reproduced or transmitted in any form or by any means, electronic or mechanical, including photocopying, recording, or by any information storage and retrieval system, without permission in writing from the copyright owner.

The views expressed in this work are solely those of the author and do not necessarily reflect the views of the publisher, and the publisher hereby disclaims any responsibility for them.

Any people depicted in stock imagery provided by Thinkstock are models, and such images are being used for illustrative purposes only.
Certain stock imagery © Thinkstock.

Print information available on the last page.

Rev. date: 25/03/2017

To order additional copies of this book, contact:
Palibrio
1663 Liberty Drive
Suite 200
Bloomington, IN 47403
Toll Free from the U.S.A 877.407.5847
Toll Free from Mexico 01.800.288.2243
Toll Free from Spain 900.866.949
From other International locations +1.812.671.9757
Fax: 01.812.355.1576
orders@palibrio.com
756114

CONTENTS

Dedication

To the memory of my grandmother Tomasa
Díaz and my father, Narciso González

For her resilience and decision to make a home in La
Frontera, where my father married my mother in 1960

For his big heart filled with humility and kindness

Enchanting Words

by Mauricio Javier González
In honor of my father and grandfather, Narciso and Andrés González

The children, barefooted and with gleaming little faces,
gathered excitedly around their father under
the crummy wooden porch.

The youngest found his lap taken and sat on the ground,
his scraped legs crossed Indian style.

With heads tilted upward and one hand under their chins,
they listened to the man whose enchanting words
did not match his ragged shirt and overalls.
Yet, the children listened like members of congress
listen to a president or parliament to a prime minister.

Only here, afterwards, the children hugged, kissed,
and climbed all over the speaker.

Introduction

The study of my father's ancestry has four main parts. Part I consists of narratives and essays that relate the events that transpired as I researched my dad's roots. They trace my steps from the time I first got the idea to take on this project. They also describe my use of microfilm to research church records without having to set foot in far-away churches. They recount my travels to Guanajuato throughout the 1990s and early 2000s. Finally, they explain how I resumed my research after relegating it for many years.

Part II includes a synopsis of the places and history surrounding the lives of my ancestors in Guanajuato. It is meant to give the reader background information to understand how the lives of my ancestors unfolded during different eras and locations. My grandparents' genealogies follow this brief history. Each ancestry begins with them and reaches as far back as the early and late 1700s, respectively. They traverse and branch out over several jurisdictions – Guanajuato, León, and Silao.

Part III is a series of photographs and facsimiles that enhances the book's content and promotes its authenticity. Most of the pictures are of me on my different trips to Guanajuato. A few are pictures from the past. They include a portrait of my paternal great-grandfather, Lucas González.

Part IV is made up of appendices, mainly family tree fan charts, that help the reader navigate the parade of names that make up the genealogies in Part II. It also includes numerous tables, which serve as visual aids.

"Map of Guanajuato"

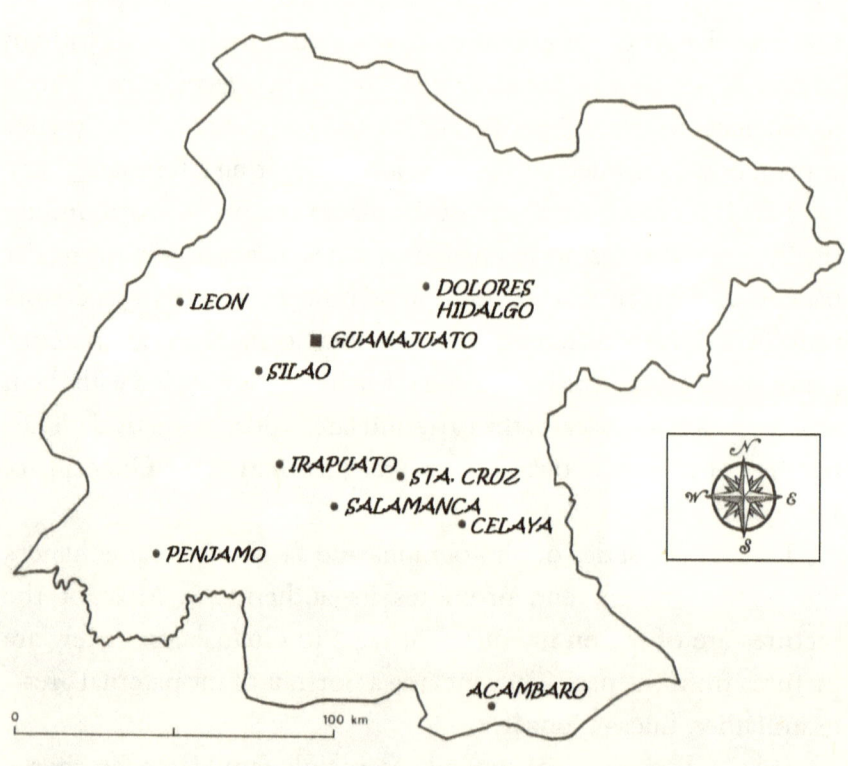

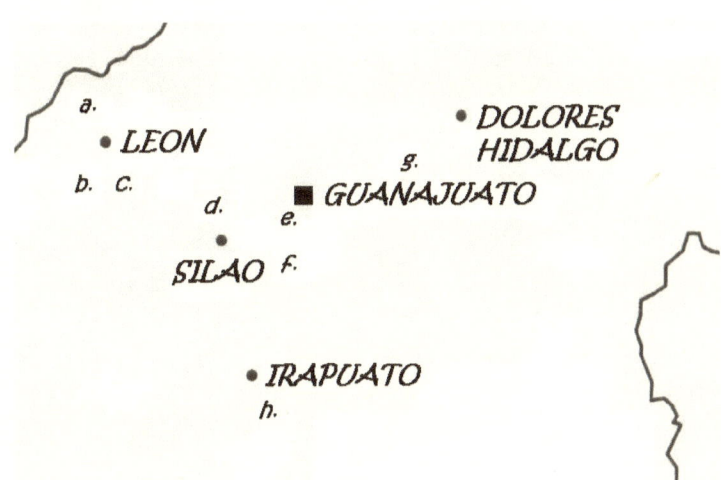

"Map of Guanajuato with Legend"

The letters on the map stand for the general location of the places listed below.

LEON
a.)
Hacienda El Palote
Hacienda Lagunillas

b.)
Hacienda San Judas (San Pedro del Monte)
Hacienda Santa Rosa

c.)
El Monte (Tepetates)

SILAO
d.)
El Coecillo (Hacienda)
San Agustín (Hacienda)

GUANAJUATO
e.)
Marfil

f.)
Cañada de Bustos
El Capulín
Hacienda de Cuevas

DOLORES HIDALGO
g.)
Cruz de Piedra

IRAPUATO
h.)
Hacienda San Roque

PART I
Narratives and Essays

How I Almost Did Not Write This Book

The idea to write a book about my father's family history first came to me in 1988. However, as I began to do research, I soon discovered that investigating my mother's side of the household was more feasible. For one thing, there were already well-established genealogical organizations dedicated to the study of the history and ancestries of families from northeastern Mexico (Coahuila, Nuevo León, and Tamaulipas) and South Texas. My mother's ancestors, who arrived in South Texas from northeastern Mexico as early as 1750, fit perfectly within the scope of research done by many genealogical societies. These included Los Bexareños Genealogical and Historical Society (San Antonio), The Spanish American Genealogical Association (Corpus Christi), Las Porciones Society (McAllen), and The Hispanic Genealogical Society of Houston. Thus, the supply and demand for such historical and genealogical studies put the necessary information at my fingertips. And although the genealogical groups' findings did not represent my entire sources, they did catapult my research and writing projects. As a consequence, I wrote and privately published three books – *Un encuentro con el pasado en San Ygnacio, Texas* (Border Studies, 1994), *The Herreras of San Ygnacio, Texas* (Border Studies, 1998), and *My Grandfather's Grandfather: Tomás Rodríguez Benavides* (Nuevo Santander Press, 2002).

Unfortunately, I did not find the same supply and demand phenomenon when it came to the history and genealogy of families of North-Central Mexico. Despite this setback, I remained curious and still wanted to investigate my father's roots. Without the aid of historical and genealogical societies like the ones mentioned here, I knew the task would be monumental. I reminded myself that I pretty much would have to start from scratch just as members of The Bexareños and other groups did beginning around 1981. And so just like these committed researchers, I sought the original sources, church records, in my case, of the state of Guanajuato. Luckily, The Church of Latter-day Saints (The Mormon Church) had already taken on the massive task of photographing church records from across the world, including Mexico. Also, they had made them accessible to the public in microfilm form. As a result, throughout the 1990s I traveled to the family history center in McAllen to view many rolls of microfilm. At the time, Laredo did not have such a facility.

After ordering and scrutinizing many reels of microfilm, I gleaned the necessary information to build strong family trees for both my parents. Nevertheless, with the investigations and publications put forth by the historical and genealogical associations, my mother's research soon surpassed my father's. What is more, as I attended several of the annual conferences hosted by the different genealogical societies (the first meeting I attended was in 1991; Las Porciones Genealogical Society of McAllen, Texas hosted it), I found myself eager to publish and share my findings. Since my mother's family history had reached different levels of completion, and most importantly, represented the societies' targeted regions for research and exposé, I concentrated my efforts on her side of the family. Not thinking I would relegate my father's study for too long, I put half of my notes in boxes and got busy writing books about my mother's ancestors.

With the hype of my three books and other projects (writing poetry), I lost track of time my father's family history had remained dormant. So caught up was I with my mother's ancestry that I even contemplated writing a fourth book on it. My dad was so proud of me for writing my books that one day he told me he had begun reading my third and most professional-looking book. It meant the world to me because I knew he was far from fluent in the English language. As a matter of fact, I never heard him pronounce a single word in English in all of my life, but I knew of his time during his youth in cities like Chicago and Milwaukee. He assured me that he understood and liked what he had read. I, of course, believed him and took his words as the ultimate compliment.

My father died in 2008 without me having written a book about his family history. As the kind person that he was, he never complained or questioned me about it. He was such the optimist that I trust he believed that one day I would. I can almost hear him say: "Nunca es tarde" (It's never too late) or "Hace más el que quiere, que el que puede" (He who wants does more than he who can. Also, where there's a will, there's a way). And as you can see by the book in your hands, my dad was right.

I Resumed My Research after Many Years

The resurgence of genealogy as an attractive hobby coincided with my decision to return to the study of my father's ancestry in 2016. Furthermore, it gave me the boost I needed not to give up. Companies like Family Tree DNA, Ancestry DNA, and 23 and Me are responsible for this trend. Using enticing ads and TV commercials, they invite the general public to perform a DNA test to learn their origins or family history. The hundreds or thousands of YouTube videos of everyday people sharing their DNA results with the world confirm how mainstream this practice has become. In the end, this phenomenon was more than enough to reignite my curiosity about my father's roots.

During the early 1990s, I found enough information on my dad's ancestors to satisfy the average family member. But I was not the average family member. I had turned into an avid researcher and student of genealogy. As a matter of fact, after I produced detailed family trees with the information I found, my relatives crowned me the family historian. However, despite the enthusiasm my findings generated, I soon hit several dead ends. Topped with the fact that my mother's ancestry found a wider audience, I soon gave up on my father's research.

The rise in popularity of DNA testing to discover your family history, which had not been available to the general public, at least not at an affordable price, gave me the stimulus I needed to continue my study. The promise of genetic genealogy to bring you closer to your ancestors was too much to resist. Nevertheless, more than advance my investigation with accurate information, DNA tests like the Autosomal or Family Finder for the most part only helped rekindle my interest. That in itself was a big deal because it prompted me to unbox my old notes on my father's ancestry.

With revitalized inspiration, I picked up where I had left off and made significant advancements in my research. In fact, by discovering one or two new generations, I was able to trace my ancestors as far back as the 1790s, something I had dreamed of doing. I made good progress on both sides of my father's family. In the end, I had enough old and new genealogical information to write a book, so I got busy writing one.

Midway writing my book I revisited a dead end in my investigation, and a sense of frustration and hopelessness invaded me. I was working on the final details of my father's direct paternal line and discovered it only went back to 1825, the year my second-to-the-last known González relative got married. Despite Nicolás González's wedding document naming his parents, I had no other proof of their existence (see Appendix II). Without other records to corroborate the information, I could only include their names as given by their son. What is worse, it meant that I could not extend their lineage any further. Nothing had changed. When it came down to the men from whom I inherited my last name and Y chromosome, I was at the same exact spot I was twenty-some years before.

Luckily, not too long after that, I had a realization, an epiphany if you will. I remembered the Y-DNA test that traces males' direct paternal lineage many generations back. Not too sure how it worked, I still submitted my DNA and got my results. Once again, the results lacked specifics, but they were enough to inject me with an invigorated curiosity that led me to persevere and score a breakthrough.

Reenergized with a new-found enthusiasm, I dove into old and new documents like a detective reopening a cold case file. I followed up on early hunches, revisited old leads, and reexamined would-be relatives I had initially dismissed. Piece by piece, I began to put together a theory and soon came to the conclusion that the Gonzalez family had moved to Silao from the next town over – León (see Map of Guanajuato). Unfortunately, Nicolás González's marriage document made no mention of this.

The breakthrough came when I examined the baptismal godparents of my known relatives' children. As an added precaution, I also tracked the sponsors and witnesses of several weddings. Soon, a network of possible relatives emerged. In the best cases, they shared a last name and place of residence. But even then, most of them led to dead ends.

In spite of my new method's lows, one name finally yielded valuable information. Josefa González was a resident of El Coecillo (in Silao's jurisdiction) just like Nicolás. She sponsored the baptisms of several children of the Quijas family, who in turn sponsored some of Nicolas'. Moreover, her son Guillermo Gómez presented three witnesses as part of his banns of marriage in 1827. Following church protocol, each witness declared under oath that he knew the groom and bride well enough to swear that they were single and lived where they said they lived. Interestingly, Guillermo's first witness, Lino Núñez, was also Nicolás'.

In the end, tracking Josefa González on a paper trail cluttered with names and dates led me to León, Guanajuato and the truth about Nicolás González's origins. As it turned out, Josefa and Nicolás González were siblings. Josefa wed Pedro Gómez in León, where her son Guillermo and her baby brother Nicolás were born in 1799. Thanks in big part to this new information I was able to trace my González lineage all the way back to the early 1700s. The details are in Part II.

The Written Legacy I Want to Leave Future Generations

I n addition to preserving the genealogical information I collected
from reading church records on microfilm, I also wanted to
gather and record the oral history my grandmother, father, and
other members of the family shared with my siblings and me. The
collection and preservation of this family lore are critical considering
that my parents, siblings, and I never visited Guanajuato as a family.
Growing up in Laredo, Texas (US), whatever we found out about
our father's birthplace, we learned through our uncles, aunts, and
cousins in Nuevo Laredo, Tamaulipas (see Appendix XI). Since my
uncle Fernando Silva still had his parents and sisters in the state of
Guanajuato, he, my aunt Fernanda, and their children made yearly
trips (sometimes more often) to León and Silao. My aunt María de
Jesús (*tía* Chuy) and her husband, Juan José González, also traveled
to Silao when my uncle's job as a truck driver required him to drive
to locations close to Guanajuato. However, their trips involving the
whole family might have been infrequent and sporadic.

For my father and aunts, who had moved to Nuevo Laredo with
their parents in the mid-1940s, traveling to Guanajuato was not as
essential. Nevertheless, this does not mean they broke all ties with
their home state. My grandmother kept in touch with her sister
Porfiria Díaz de Caudillo and visited her at Cañada de Bustos on a
regular basis. As a devoted Catholic, she also made pilgrimages to
San Juan de Los Lagos (Jalisco), La Basílica (Mexico City), and El
Cubilete (Guanajuato). Her trips must have been frequent especially
when she owned property. At one time it included the two lots where

my aunts built their homes after they got married, the piece of land she donated to La Parroquia de Nuestra Señora del Carmen, and a modest apartment complex a few blocks away from where she lived. My father and my aunt Inocencia, the youngest members of the family, accompanied my grandmother on some of her trips.

While our cousins learned about their connection to Guanajuato during their travels with their parents starting in the 1950s, my siblings and I did not catch up until the 1980s. By then, we were interested and old enough to take it upon ourselves to finally get to know SILAO – our father's birthplace. It started when my sister Guillermina and her husband, Eduardo, visited my cousin Juan José González II in Celaya. By this time, our cousin Juan had become a school teacher in Tamaulipas and had been assigned to teach in the state of Guanajuato. I followed in my sister's footsteps in 1992. Already immersed in the study of my father's family history, I spent every day of my week-long trip visiting and interviewing relatives.

I returned many times to Guanajuato, including in 1994 when my father accompanied my sisters Gricelda, Guillermina, and me on a fantastic trip to his homeland. My sisters and I returned again in 1996. On that occasion, some of our children and my wife, Marina, went with us. In 1997, I traveled to Guanajuato with my cousin Víctor González, his wife, Isabel, and their two daughters. We spent New Year's Eve with his brother, Juan José, in Celaya. I made two additional trips, one in 2000 and another in 2002. Only my brother, Narciso González II, has yet to travel to Guanajuato.

My cousin Juan José was fundamental in all of our trips to Guanajuato. Together with his wife, Ana, and their children at the time, Juan José III and Claudia, he welcomed us into his home. Also, he facilitated the visits we paid our new-found relatives across the state, which advanced my research tremendously. We will always be grateful to our cousin and his family for their hospitality.

From a tourist's point of view, our trips to Guanajuato were full of surprises and new experiences. My family members and I reveled in the many attractions colonial cities like Celaya, Salamanca, Irapuato, Silao, León, and the capital city of Guanajuato have to offer. Still, I never forgot my commitment to the study of my ancestors and always made it a point to visit the places where they had lived.

I Fell in Love with My Heritage

As I became familiarized with Guanajuato and its history, a sense of pride came over me. As a result, I wanted to surround myself with everything related to my ancestors' homeland. I sought books, movies, songs, and even clothes that manifested, in one way or another, Guanajuato's rich culture and history.

Among the first things I did was buy a serape. I was proud I had bought it in Guanajuato. As I paid the man who sold it to me, I could not help stare at him for a moment. It was my first trip to Guanajuato, and I thought I saw my ancestors in the people at the *mercados* (markets), restaurants, and on the streets. I remember thinking that any one of them could be my relative. The whole experience was new and strange to me. Once in Laredo, I wore my serape to a get-together. I thought it was the coolest thing until my friend pulled me to the side and said, "I think you better take it off." I understood what he meant and removed it. I still laugh whenever I think about it, but it just shows how infatuated I was with Guanajuato.

However, nothing I did showed my fascination with Guanajuato more than the reverence I felt for José Alfredo Jiménez. And even though I found out that Diego Rivera, Pedro Vargas, Jorge Negrete, and other celebrities from the past were also from Guanajuato, José Alfredo Jiménez became my absolute favorite. His songs, several of which refer to Guanajuato and its people, filled me with extreme pride. I still recall driving back to Laredo from the family history center in McAllen with only José Alfredo's songs as my companions.

It was an awesome feeling when I made a discovery in my genealogy, and José Alfredo was there to celebrate with me. Songs like "Camino de Guanajuato" and "15 de septiembre," were among my favorite at the time.

Lines from CAMINO DE GUANAJUATO

Bonito León Guanajuato / allá en mi León Guanajuato /el Cristo de tu montaña / el Cerro del Cubilete /camino de Guanajuato / no pases por Salamanca /la Sierra de Guanajuato /se ve Dolores Hidalgo

Lines from 15 DE SEPTIEMBRE

Ese pueblo de Dolores, qué pueblito /Guanajuato está orgulloso de tener entre su estado /cuna de la independencia, alma de nuestra nación /es el día que celebramos lo que Hidalgo principió /que repiquen las campanas de Dolores

Adopting José Alfredo Jiménez as my favorite music artist also meant that I played his music at most, if not all, of our family gatherings. Consequently, when someone was asked to guess my favorite singer, they knew who to name. His music was so prevalent in my home and car that my family members soon preferred him as well. There was a time when all the music I heard belonged to José Alfredo.

My Ancestors' Places of Origin Up-Close

The study of my ancestors took me on two important journeys. The first, which I have hinted at in an earlier section, took me down a paper trail many generations long. Symbolically, it brought me face to face with my ancestors. As I read their names on old church records at a Texas family history center equipped with microfilm readers, I felt that I was meeting them. Reading their names under my breath in awe was the equivalent of setting my eyes on their actual person. Learning their ages, occupations, and places of residence was like having a conversation with them. The whole experience was surreal and incredibly unique. I still recall getting lost in thought and feeling like an archaeologist making significant discoveries. Only here, the fossils or relics uncovered were ordinary people. However, put in the right context, they were nothing short than giants in a progression of generations and ancestors that made up my family tree.

As extraordinary as this journey was, it was a process more than 25 years in the making. It started when my grandmother Tomasa Díaz (González) passed away at her home in Nuevo Laredo, in 1988. Her death led to several legalities, including a death certificate which prompted documents with her personal information to surface. Somehow I managed to read one of them and was both baffled and intrigued by the names on it. I remember regretting not being able to ask my grandmother who they were. Still, I wanted to know.

Learning the names of my grandmother's parents in 1988 was just the beginning. Soon I committed myself to finding out more and immersed myself in genealogy. What happened next I covered in a previous section.

My second journey consisted of my travels to different cities, towns, former haciendas, and ranchos in Guanajuato. There I got the chance to meet new-found relatives and see the places my ancestors called home for many generations. I had already learned my forebears' names by reading old church records hundreds of miles away from Guanajuato. It was only befitting that I pay tribute to them by setting foot on their native land.

Silao, Guanajuato

Silao, Guanajuato, my grandfather's birthplace, was no doubt at the center of my study of his side of the family (see Map of Guanajuato). It was there that I met my aunts Rafaela and Guadalupe Montes (see Appendix XII). I met them on my first trip to Guanajuato in March of 1992. That visit represented one of two times I talked to my aunt Rafaela, the older of the two sisters. Among the most memorable things she told me was how the Santo Cristo (the 3-foot-tall Christ on the cross figure in my parents' home in Laredo, Texas) had belonged to her grandmother María de Jesús Reyes. According to Rafaela, the Christ figure had been part of grand religious processions. Her son Manuel Montes was present the day of the conversation.

My aunt Guadalupe, whom I ended up having more contact with, helped me obtain additional information on the González family. First, she provided me with details about our family history. Second, she advised me on where to go and whom to talk to, to find information. She even gave me plenty of directions to move around Silao like a local. Thanks to her guidance I was able to visit the city cemetery, the library inside La Casa de la Cultura, El Archivo Histórico inside City Hall (*Presidencia Municipal*), the home of Silao's historian (Margarito Vázquez Navarro), and La Parroquia de Santiago Apóstol. Finally, as my contact person and guide, she introduced me to other relatives in Silao's jurisdiction.

Thanks to my aunt Guadalupe *(tia* Lupe) I was able to visit San Agustín, a former hacienda north of Silao (see Map of Guanajuato). San Agustín has been the home of the Gonzálezes for many generations. When I arrived in 1996, it was home to the descendants of Amado González (see Appendix XII). I met Agustín González's family. Although Agustín had already passed away, his widow, Josefina Camarillo, was there to meet us. I remember her conversation starting with how her husband and son had drowned in a river just a few years earlier – father trying to save his son. She also told us that she had arrived in San Agustín around the time Amado González died.

According to a census, in 1930, Amado lived in San Agustín with his wife, Gregoria, his son Rosalío, and his daughter-in-law, Sancha Sauceda. There was also Agustín (age 15) and Arcadio (age 12), Rosalío and Sancha's sons. Amado's daughter, Micaela González, and her husband, Genaro Sánchez, also resided in San Agustín.

Agustín and Josefina became a couple soon after she arrived in San Agustín. According to Josefina, she and her husband were close to my grandparents, so much that they served as my aunt Inocencia's baptismal sponsors in 1936. Josefina recalled that her husband called my grandfather, *tio* (uncle).

I visited San Agustín again in 2002. While waiting in downtown Silao for the bus that took me there, I met a man from San Agustín named Odilón Trejo. Odilón was 73 years old and knew Amado González's family well. Although I asked him different questions, his conversation centered on Rosalío González, Amado's son. Rosalío, it turned out, had many enemies due to his rebellious nature and bravado. As a consequence, he was ambushed by his foes one evening as he rode on horseback. When I got to San Agustín, I brought up what Odilón had told me. Josefina's silence seemed to confirm what he had said.

Josefina took me to meet two of her sons. One of them was working in a small field along the dirt road we were taking. He stopped to acknowledge us and then went back to work. I remember that he resembled my father. Further up the road, we went to her second son's house. Only his wife and some of his children were there. Pressed for time (I needed to catch the last bus back to Silao), I told them who I was and left without meeting my uncle. Back at her place, Josefina mentioned her son Filiberto. He had left San Agustín to find work in the United States and seldom wrote to her. Her daughter-in-law Herminia, whose husband had drowned along with his father, was present. According to her, Filiberto headed to Laredo. I felt sorry for Josefina, who started weeping as she spoke about her son.

I will always be grateful to Josefina for making me feel welcome during my two visits to San Agustín. Despite her limited resources, she was a gracious hostess. There is no doubt that under her little and fragile frame was a big heart. I am lucky to have met her. When it was time to say our goodbyes, I asked Josefina to pose with me for a picture (see Photographs and Facsimiles). Thinking about where to take it, we finally stood near a massive tree in front of her house. As her daughter-in-law prepared to snap the shot, Josefina told me that the enormous tree had been there since before she arrived in San Agustín. That meant it was probably there when my great-grandfather Lucas González and his brother Amado were still alive. I was overwhelmed.

My aunt Lupe also helped me locate a photograph of my great-grandfather Lucas González (see Photographs and Facsimiles). It started with her conversation of how her sister Rafaela had seen a picture of Lucas when she visited family in Pomona, California. I had no idea where Pomona was or who her relatives were, but I instantly knew I had to see that photograph. The relatives she had referred to were the children of Preciliana González (see Appendix XII). Preciliana and her husband, Mucio Zúñiga, had settled in

Southern California. According to Rafaela, the picture was handed down from Preciliana to one of her children to José Natividad Montes, who lived in Pomona at the time. Preciliana's daughters or *Las Tías* Zúñiga (as my aunt Lupe called them) included Carmen, María, Aurora, and Juana. Carmen and María shared a home in Pomona. Aurora or Juana, whose husband's last name is Ortiz, lived in Oxnard. Their brother Francisco owned a restaurant in Pomona, where he lived with his wife, Rebeca.

I did not meet *Los Zúñiga* in person, but I did get to speak to them on the phone. I talked to Francisco while I was in California. Sometime after I got back to Laredo, I called Carmen and María. I was both amazed and surprised when the older of the two told me the name of Lucas González's father – Plácido González. I had already discovered the name myself, but I believe that if I had not, my joy would have been just as great as when I read his name on a church record for the first time. I doubt that either one was old enough to have met him, which means that their mother must have talked to them about their grandfather and family history in general.

According to Josefina Camarillo, Preciliana made occasional trips to Silao and San Agustín. Josefina recalled the bundles of clothes she brought her and her family. Preciliana was much younger than her older brothers, Lucas and Amado. Lucas, who was the oldest of the three, was 22 years her senior (see Appendix XII).

The trail leading to Lucas González's photograph took me to José Natividad's widow, María del Socorro Padilla, and their son Víctor Manuel Montes, who had recently relocated to Fontana from Pomona. After I introduced myself to Víctor on the phone and made the necessary arrangements to meet him in person, I took a plane to Ontario, California, in 1996. Once in Fontana, Víctor and his mother showed me Lucas' photo, and to my surprise, let me keep it. I will always be grateful to Víctor, his mother, wife (Ana Alcalá), and children for their hospitality and generosity.

Víctor and I got along as if we had known each other for a long time. As his mother informed me, we almost did. It turned out that before calling California home, Víctor's parents arrived in Nuevo Laredo as newlyweds. It happened in 1949 when Víctor was just a few months old. Víctor's father, José Natividad Montes, had picked Nuevo Laredo as their new home because his uncle Andrés and aunts San Juana and Luz lived there. However, when Víctor started falling ill, and a doctor suggested it might be something in the air, his parents returned to Silao and later looked at Pomona as an alternative place to start a life together. When I mentioned this story to my aunt Inocencia in Nuevo Laredo, she recalled how her cousin and his wife left the city abruptly, also how my grandparents returned the couple's unpaid furniture to a furniture maker after it arrived at their house.

In all, I visited my aunt Lupe four times – in 1992, 1996, 1997, and 2000. When I traveled to Guanajuato with my father in 1994, we stopped by Silao, but my aunt was not home. When I returned in 2002 (my last trip to Guanajuato), she had already passed away. I will always be grateful to my aunt for taking the time to talk to me. I could not always let her know I was dropping by, but she always made me feel welcome at her home near the corner of Madero and Cinco de Mayo Street.

Cañada de Bustos

Cañada de Bustos (from now on Cañada) was the most significant place in the study of my grandmother Tomasa Díaz (see Map of Guanajuato). Not surprisingly, it was the first place (related to her) I visited during my first trip to Guanajuato in 1992. To begin with, it was where my grandmother grew up. Although she was born in Rancho Nuevo, a short distance from Cañada, Cañada had always been her family's home base. Also, it was the most mentioned place in all the records I studied.

Cañada is a small community with homes on opposite sides of a ravine (*cañada*) that cuts and snakes through the area from one end to the other. When I naively asked my uncle Fernando Silva in Nuevo Laredo for directions (streets and such) to get to the home of my uncle and guide, Ignacio Caudillo, he chuckled (see Appendices XI & XIII). It was his way of letting me know that Cañada was not a town, but a hamlet. I later found out that besides the walking paths leading to people's homes, there was only one dirt road for vehicles.

After my uncle Ignacio Caudillo (*tío* Nacho) and I introduced each other and became acquainted, he took me to meet Isidro Díaz, my grandmother's cousin. How can I forget the encounter! I still recall the scent of burned *mazorcas de maíz* (corn) in the air, the narrow twisting trail going down and up the ravine that led us to his adobe home, the donkey eating hay in the yard, and his wife on her death bed. I was excited to meet him but extremely saddened and confused by his wife's condition. Despite our heavy hearts, we managed to talk a little about our ancestors. On a subsequent visit to Cañada, I met at least one more elderly family member, this time on my grandmother's maternal side – Silva. Isidro Díaz had died by then. I remember thinking his cause of death must have been sorrow and loneliness.

All in all, I visited Cañada three times. In 1994, my father accompanied me. It was special to see him interact with his cousin Ignacio Caudillo, whom he had not seen in many years. As I found out, my uncle Nacho had visited my grandmother and her family in Nuevo Laredo as a young man. My dad, in turn, had traveled to Cañada, also in his youth. He once told me that he attended a wedding there with my grandmother, and a young lady asked him if she could go with them to La Frontera (The Border). He also recalled that relatives and friends had greeted my grandmother with a grand feast. My father was obviously impressed by how people from Cañada and beyond esteemed his mother. "They must have killed their fattest pig for her," he said.

My research also took me to El Capulín and Cuevas nearby. El Capulín is south of and similar to Cañada, so much that they could be considered sister communities. My ancestors probably did because they moved back and forth between the two. Cuevas is a former hacienda north of Cañada. It is significant because some of my ancestors from there married my ancestors from Cañada and El Capulín. Also, Cuevas represents a place with a long and rich history.

My trip to my ancestors' homeland would not have been complete without me traveling to the cities of Guanajuato and Marfil, northwest of Cañada and Cuevas (see Map of Guanajuato). Guanajuato is not only the capital of the state and a major tourist destination but also where I did research at the Archivo General del Gobierno del Estado de Guanajuato. Marfil is special because it is the home of the Parroquia de San José y Santiago. I was lucky to visit the church and see firsthand where my ancestors joined in holy matrimony and christened their children over several centuries.

León, Guanajuato

When I traveled to León in 1992 and 1994, I did not know I had ancestors who had lived there (see Map of Guanajuato). That information I only found out in 2016. Learning that my González lineage had a strong presence in León throughout the 1700s filled me with ecstasy and pride. León, the state of Guanajuato's largest city and Mexico's fourth, is renowned for its leather industry, which attracts national and international markets for its manufacturing of shoes, boots, belts, jackets, and other leather accessories. Not surprisingly, the city was dubbed *Perla del Bajío* (Pearl of the Lowlands) and *Capital Mundial de la Piel y del Calzado* (Leather and Footwear Capital of the World).

León's legacy in the production of shoes has deep roots. In 1719, when León's population was around 3,000 inhabitants, the occupation of *zapatero* (shoemaker or cobbler) ranked number one out of 18 trades. There were 67 shoemakers compared to 38 *arrieros* (muleteers), which came in in second place (Brading 93). In 1792, something similar registered in nearby Silao. 40 shoemakers outnumbered 27 muleteers. However, the occupation of shoemaker was not the most popular. It ranked fourth after *labradores, comerciantes,* and *sastres* (farmworkers, merchants, and tailors) (Vázquez 351). My grandfather Andrés González was a *zapatero* by trade. I wonder if he followed in any of our ancestors' footsteps.

Just as important, I am proud of my connection with León, Guanajuato because José Alfredo Jiménez made the city emblematic when he incorporated it into his song "Camino de Guanajuato."

> *Bonito León Guanajuato*
> *su feria con su jugada*
> *ahí se apuesta la vida*
> *y se respeta al que gana*
> *allá en mi León Guanajuato*
> *la vida no vale nada*

While in León, I bought a beautiful leather jacket at a *mercado* (market) (see Photographs and Facsimiles). To say I was mesmerized by the quantity and assortment of leather products sold there would be an understatement. In downtown León, I visited an area closed to vehicular traffic known as *Zona Peatonal* (Pedestrian Zone). There tourists can stroll at their leisure and enjoy the sights of León's historical center, such as La Plaza de Los Fundadores (The Founders' Square). This beautiful and open space is home to some of the city's iconic symbols, including La Fuente de Los Leones (The Lions' Fountain).

My first trip to León in 1992 was more about meeting relatives than going sightseeing. On that occasion, I met Luz Silva and his wife, Aurelia Barrientos. They were originally from Cañada de

Bustos and represented my grandmother's side of the family. Luz Silva was my grandmother's cousin.

My González ancestors from León moved to Silao in the early 1800s. Finding the descendants of any ancestor that remained in León would have been a monumental task. However, with DNA tests available today, this might no longer be the case. As a matter of fact, after doing a Y-DNA test, I found out I share the same Y chromosome (the one passed down from father to son) with one or two individuals registered in a genetic genealogy database. I know that at least one of them is from Guanajuato. With any luck, he just might be from León.

My Grandfather Andrés González

My grandfather Andrés González was born in Silao, Guanajuato to Lucas González and María de Jesús Reyes on November 7, 1892.

In Silao, he reached young adulthood and married my grandmother Tomasa Díaz. According to relatives, he courted her while she sold goods from a basket at a local market. It must have happened before 1919, the year their eldest daughter, Florencia, was born. Their other children included María de Jesús, Cándido, Fernanda, Narciso (my father), and Inocencia (see Appendix XII).

According to a census, in 1930, my grandparents lived with their children near the corner of Aurora and Esperanza Street. Florencia was 11 years old while Fernanda, the youngest member of the family at the time, was two. My father was not listed because he was born one year later. The census was reportedly taken in May and did not include my grandfather's mother, María de Jesús Reyes, who died on April 26, 1930.

When María de Jesús passed away, my grandfather told authorities that she had died at home of enteritis. The death record did not specify if my grandparents and María de Jesús lived together even though my grandmother used to say she cared for her in her old age. Still, my grandfather gave his address as 68 Arenal Street.

At the time of her demise, no one knew the names of María de Jesús' parents. She had become an orphan at a very young age. My grandmother too had lost her mother as a child. Perhaps this shared misfortune was what led her to care for her mother-in-law. It would explain why my grandfather, and not his sisters, was the informant of his mother's passing. Whether María de Jesús' home was on Arenal or Aurora Street is unknown.

My grandparents later moved to Aldama Street. It was around this time that Florencia González died as a teenager. This new address was their third address in just a few years (see Appendix XIV). Family members I talked to knew about my grandparents' time on Aurora and Aldama Street, but not Arenal Street. They were either too young or not alive when it happened.

Aurora and Aldama Street run close and parallel to each other east of downtown Silao. Arenal Street is several blocks to the south. In 1992, I went to Aldama Street, where my aunt Guadalupe Montes used to visit her uncle Andrés and aunt Tomasa in the 1930s and 40s. Unfortunately, people were living in my grandparents' former home, and I could not explore it. In the end, we did not spend too much time there, so my memory of the house is vague.

Luckily, years later my aunt Lupe shared her recollection of the inside of my grandparents' home. She described an entrance way *(portalito)* that led to a first room followed by another. Making gestures with her hands, she also described the little kitchen and finally the backyard where my grandfather kept his two light grey donkeys in a corral. The family (nieces included) would ride them on their frequent trips to La Montaña del Cubilete (a religious site consisting of a colossal statue of El Cristo Rey, or Christ the King, atop a big hill). My aunt fondly recalled the time my grandmother fell off one of the donkeys on their way up. They also made occasional jaunts to nearby Aguas Buenas, where they bathed in natural hot springs.

My aunt also remembered my grandfather's tools strewn about his workspace at home. As a *zapatero* (shoe cobbler), he had a cast iron shoe and all sort of pliers. According to my father, my grandfather had a steady clientele, but his drinking never allowed him to save or invest the money he earned. As a consequence, my grandmother had to work in the fields and help her husband put food on the table. Rafael Mármol and Sóstenes Martínez were fellow *zapateros* and friends of my grandfather. Rafael resided on Lucero Avenue, which runs perpendicular to Aurora and Aldama Street. Sóstenes lived on Aldama Street. Rafael and Sóstenes were witnesses to María de Jesús' demise in 1930.

In 2002, I visited Aurora Street after I met and spoke with Silao's historian, Margarito Vázquez Navarro. He told me that Jorge Negrete, the singer and movie star (1911-1953), had lived on Aurora Street as a child. It happened because his mother was a native of Silao. Margarito maintained that Negrete was probably born in Silao, where his mother's closest female relatives would have been at her side during childbirth. He believed that Guanajuato was recorded as Negrete's birthplace since it represented a more prominent place. After all, Negrete was the son of a high-ranking military officer, and Guanajuato, due to its glorious mining past, was a city known the world over.

As I walked along Aurora Street, there was no one to help me identify my grandparents' former residence. Even my aunt Lupe could not give me a hand. She had passed away a year or two earlier. I did, however, come across Negrete's late home. It had a plaque on the outer wall commemorating the years the movie star lived there.

My grandparents left Guanajuato in the mid-1940s. They had received news of job opportunities in La Frontera (The Border) from my great-aunt Luz González (see Appendix XII). Looking to improve their quality of life, they moved to Tamaulipas. According to my aunt Lupe, after my grandparents put up their home for sale, my grandmother went to ask for her *madrina* (godmother) Porfiria's blessing. Porfiria was the woman who had sheltered my grandmother in her time of need. There is more on this subject in the next section. After this and other arrangements, my grandparents said goodbye to their homeland and started a new chapter in their lives in the city of Nuevo Laredo.

My Grandmother Tomasa Díaz

My grandmother Tomasa Díaz was born in Rancho Nuevo (near Cañada de Bustos) to Eulogio Díaz and Teresa Silva in 1899. Porfiria and Marcelina Díaz were her two older sisters.

I remember my grandmother telling my family that she was born *con el siglo* (with the century). I suppose the year 1900 was her way of remembering her birth year. According to her baptismal document, my grandmother's actual name was Mauricia Bruna. A notation on the certificate states that Tomasa and Mauricia Bruna were one and the same. It also reveals that my grandmother acquired the document in Marfil, Guanajuato on January 30, 1945.

My grandmother and her sisters faced many hardships after their mother died and their father remarried. To begin with, they received harsh treatment from their stepmother. Also, with the advent of the Revolutionary War during the first decade of the 1900s, they suffered the threat of violence and a shortage of food. My grandmother once told me that starvation was so real she once had to eat the straw off a broom. Also, according to my father, my grandmother had to be lowered down a well to hide from revolutionaries during one or more raids.

Amid or after the turmoil caused by the war, my grandmother and her sisters went their separate ways. Porfiria, who had been taken in by Germán Silva (the girls' maternal grandfather) at about one year old, remained at Cañada de Bustos (see Appendix VI). There she eventually met and married Apolonio Caudillo. In 1930, their children included Emilia (age 8), Catalina (age 6), Antolino (age 4), and Ignacio (age 2), (see Appendix XIII). Marcelina wed Francisco Bustos and left Guanajuato. In the 1930s and 1940s, the couple lived in Lockhart, Texas. In 1940, their children were Francisco, Trinidad (Trino), Eduardo (Lalo), Joaquina, Julio, Trinidad (Trine), and Felisa. Julio and Felisa passed away in 1942 and 1948, respectively. Their daughter Loreta had died in 1939. By the late 1940s, the family resided in Hidalgo County in the Pharr/McAllen area.

My grandmother ended up in the care of Doña Porfiria, a wealthy woman from Silao. Doña Porfiria was known as my grandmother's *madrina* (godmother) even though her actual baptismal sponsors were Ambrosio Olmos and Refugio Venegas. Perhaps in their case, the title of "madrina" symbolically stood for a foster parent.

According to my aunt Guadalupe Montes, my grandmother found refuge with Doña Porfiria after she ran away from home due to a scuffle with her stepmother. It started when my grandmother defended one of her siblings (most likely her younger sister) from her stepmother and got hit in the head pretty badly. "It was the last straw," my grandmother told my aunt Lupe many years after.

In 2000, I finally made plans to see where my grandmother had lived with her protector, Doña Porfiria, but it was too late. The local government had the house demolished one year earlier. Apparently, years after Porfiria passed away, the municipality took possession of the property. During that period, at least one person, Santiago Blancarte, rented the place. Don Chago, as Santiago was known, set up a carpentry shop and worked there for many years. In 1976, a great flood devastated the city of Silao and left the house in shambles. That is how people remember it today.

By the time of my visit, the only vestige of the former two-story mansion was part of its foundation partially sticking out of the ground. Lying parallel to Cinco de Mayo Avenue, the dark brownish stone blocks were an awkward component of a modest public garden (*jardín*). In 2012, city officials upgraded the garden to a park named after Felice Bonetto, the Italian international auto race car driver.

Bonetto crashed his car and died in Silao during the Pan American Race of 1953. The tragic accident, which occurred precisely on Cinco de Mayo Avenue, brought Silao a lot of publicity.

While in Silao, my grandmother met and married my grandfather Andrés González. They raised a family and lived in Silao until they relocated to Tamaulipas in the mid-1940s.

PART II

History and Genealogies

The Places and History Surrounding
The Lives of My Ancestors in Guanajuato

My grandparents were from neighboring jurisdictions in the state of Guanajuato. My grandfather Andrés was born and raised in Silao, the seat of the municipality and the only city in the district. My grandmother hailed from Cañada de Bustos in Guanajuato's jurisdiction. The two territories meet where the Sierra de Guanajuato flattens and gives way to *los llanos* (the plains) of Irapuato, Silao, and León. While Guanajuato's district is mostly mountainous, Silao's is part of *El Bajío* (The Lowlands).

As a result, there were two main types of haciendas and ranchos in the region. In the hilly terrain of Guanajuato's district, there were haciendas *de beneficio* (smelters). These haciendas acted as refineries of the precious metals (gold, silver, and copper) extracted from the mines. Using different methods, crews of workers utilized water, fire, and other means to process the raw material. It was a system and a way of life that had made Guanajuato one the wealthiest cities in New Spain (Mexico). At one time, Guanajuato produced one-fourth of the world's silver.

Most haciendas on the fertile plains of Silao, León, and Irapuato were haciendas *de campo* (field estates). Their mission was the production of corn, wheat, and other crops. They also raised cattle and work animals. More than satisfy the local residents' consumption, these haciendas supplied the city of Guanajuato with foodstuffs and beasts of burden on a massive scale. Consequently, when the general population and mining workforce swelled, the haciendas' operations became indispensable to the survival of the people and the mines.

The production at these agricultural and ranching centers was so prosperous that they also supplied Mexico City and Puebla with corn, wheat, and beans.

Depending on the period my ancestors lived in, they had different experiences on these haciendas and ranchos. Those alive during the 1700s, when the mines were at their peak, would have had plenty of job opportunities. These would have ranged from mining to tending crops and livestock.

Hacienda de Cuevas in Guanajuato's jurisdiction was one of several haciendas where my ancestors lived and worked during the 1700s (see Map of Guanajuato). In addition to having a long and rich history, Cuevas stood out because it was both a smelter and field estate. Its size and location must have afforded its owners both industries. Hacienda de Santiago, Hacienda del Chapín, Rancho de la Peña Caída, and Ranchito de la Piedad represent other haciendas and ranchos in Guanajuato's district where my ancestors resided and labored. In León and its surroundings, my ancestors spent their lives on Hacienda de Sánchez, Hacienda de Santa Rosa, Hacienda El Palote, Pueblo del Coecillo, San Judas, and Del Monte. In Silao and Irapuato, they were present in Haciendas El Coecillo and San Roque, respectively.

The next generations of my ancestors had an entirely different experience. The War of Independence (1810-1821), which originated in the state of Guanajuato, brought turmoil and calamity to the region. As insurgents and royalist troops clashed in military campaigns that sucked the life out of communities, daily life and business were crippled. As a result, a shortage of food and work plagued many jurisdictions. To make matters worse, the people also had to contend with war-related atrocities. As the fighting and carnage intensified, many families fled, leaving behind a scene of disaster and desolation.

The mines and haciendas also suffered the effects of the war. Miners and hacienda workers disbanded, either to run for their lives or to join the fight. If this did not render the mines and haciendas useless, the damage to their infrastructures did. Consequently, many of their owners halted or abandoned their enterprises for good.

The following generations did not fare well either. After Mexico won its Independence from Spain in 1821, the newly-formed Mexican government remained unstable for decades to come. As conservatives and liberals battled for power, the inhabitants of Guanajuato lived in fear as leaders from both groups threatened to attack and take over the capital city of Guanajuato as a sign of victory. As if this were not enough, other conflicts that affected Guanajuato in one way or another followed: the first French intervention of 1838-1839, the Reform War or Mexican Civil War of 1857-1861, the French intervention in Mexico of 1861-1867, etc. Needless to say, any warfare brought the townspeople of Guanajuato and the surrounding districts misery, desolation, and despair. Finally, epidemics of smallpox, measles, and cholera were also calamities the people of the time had to contend with, and Guanajuato had its share of each in the 1800s. "1850 — Marzo. Invade por segunda vez el cólera morbus a Guanajuato. Sus estragos aunque terribles fueron menores que en 1833." (1850 — March. Cholera morbus invades Guanajuato for the second time. Its ravages while terrible were lower than in 1833.) (Marmolejo 287)

As a result of further warfare, epidemics, and flooding (due to prolonged mining activity near rivers), more haciendas and ranchos were downgraded or shut down. With so many laborers out of work, the economy inevitably suffered. "La actividad de Silao quedó paralizada" (Silao's activity was paralyzed) (Vázquez 91). Consequently, the people turned to contained farming as their primary means of employment and personal subsistence. In so doing, they rendered many haciendas and ranchos obsolete. The age of supplying the opulent capital city of Guanajuato with agricultural products and beasts of burden had ended.

A list of haciendas and ranchos that were home to my ancestors during the mid and late 1800s follows. In the district of Guanajuato, there were Cañada de Bustos, El Capulín, Rancho de la Soledad, and former Hacienda de Cuevas. In Silao's jurisdiction, there were two neighboring old haciendas – El Coecillo and San Agustín – and a farming community called La Laborcita (de López).

In the last stage or period in the lives of my ancestors, there was the brutal and chaotic Mexican Revolution (1910 – 1920). In an attempt to remove Porfirio Díaz from his dictatorship (1876-1911) and balance the distribution of power, wealth, and land in Mexico, revolutionaries like Pancho Villa, Emiliano Zapata, and Francisco Madero brought war and upheaval to the nation, including Guanajuato. How this war affected my ancestors is described in some of the pages ahead.

Andrés González's Parents

Lucas González was born in San Agustín (in Silao's jurisdiction) on October 17, 1859. He wed **María de Jesús Reyes** in the parish church in Silao, on January 10, 1887. María de Jesús was from Silao. Her parents had already passed away by the time of her wedding (see Appendix I).

According to his marriage document, Lucas was a *jornalero* (day laborer). My aunt Guadalupe Montes once told me that Lucas worked for the Macías or Morado family on Hacienda de Chichimequillas, north of San Agustín (see Map of Guanajuato). She had heard this from a long-time friend of the González family called Chonita.

Lucas and María de Jesús' other children included María Natividad, Magdaleno, San Juana, and María de la Luz (see Appendix XII). María Natividad married Manuel Montes. In 1930, the couple lived in Silao with their four offspring, Soledad (age 14), José Natividad (age 10), Rafaela (age 4), and Guadalupe (age 1). Magdaleno left home as a teenager around 1915. His family never heard from him again. My aunts Rafaela and Guadalupe could tell me only two things about him. First, his mother, María de Jesús, had cried incessantly for his absence. Second, he might have headed to either Ciudad Juárez or Piedras Negras. San Juana and María de la Luz married their respective husbands and settled in Nuevo Laredo, Tamaulipas.

In 1991, I asked my aunt Luz González at her home in Nuevo Laredo about her father, Lucas. She told me that he had died in Irapuato when she was just a little girl. She insisted that he had gone there in search of something. She could not explain what it was and only said it must have been some object, perhaps a tool or implement. She and her mother had been at his side.

My aunt Luz was always an excellent hostess to me. She also helped me contact my aunts Rafaela and Guadalupe Montes (Las Montes, as she referred to them) in Silao. I will always be grateful to her.

María de Jesús Reyes died in Silao in 1930. The details are in a previous section. Lucas perished in the mid or late 1910s.

Andrés González's Paternal Grandparents

L *ucas González's* parents, **Plácido González** and **Gregoria Velásquez**, wed in the parish church in Silao, on December 1, 1854. They were 20 and 17 years old, respectively, and resided in La Laborcita. Both their parents were alive at the time (see Appendix I).

La Laborcita was most likely east of San Agustín, a former hacienda *de campo* (field estate) (see Map of Guanajuato). According to *Estadística General de la República Mexicana*, San Agustín had 321 inhabitants in 1887. La Laborcita had only 49 (Peñafiel 173 & 175).

When Plácido's brother Domingo married Crisanta Juárez in 1850, he was a resident of San Agustín. However, as he and his wife welcomed their children into the world, they moved between La Labor de Aguas Buenas, La Laborcita (de López), and San Agustín (see Appendix XV).

Plácido and Gregoria's address also changed during the years. La Laborcita was their home when they wed and also when they baptized their daughter Cayetana in 1857. Nevertheless, when their other children were born between 1859 and 1881, their place of residence was San Agustín.

Plácido's other brother, Pedro González, married Juana Hernández. When the couple christened their daughter María Teresa in 1857, the family lived in San Agustín.

As shown by Plácido and his brothers, San Agustín and La Laborcita were an integral part of the González family. Despite their parents residing at El Coecillo, the brothers made a home and living in these two communities.

Plácido and Gregoria's other children included Amado, Romana, and Preciliana. Amado and Preciliana have been discussed in a different section (see My Ancestors' Places of Origin Up-Close). Romana was born in 1876. She left Guanajuato for Ciudad Juárez, Chihuahua.

Andrés González's Paternal
Great-Grandparents

*P*lácido González's parents, **Nicolás González** and **Luisa Hernández**, wed in the parish church in Silao, in 1825. At the time, Nicolás and Luisa were residents of El Coecillo, a hacienda north of Silao with a long history (see Map of Guanajuato). Nicolás' parents had already passed away. Luisa's were still alive (see Appendices II & III).

Luisa's parents lived in Silao, where she was born in 1810. Nicolás moved to Silao's district from León. He arrived at El Coecillo with his older sister, Josefa González, and her children. Exactly when is unknown. It is also unknown if their parents and Josefa's husband, Pedro Gómez, were at their side.

If Nicolás and his family arrived before 1810, then they witnessed the first attempt to make Mexico independent from Spain. It happened in Silao's jurisdiction in 1808. As a result, they must have noticed their neighbors act nervous and restless, and with good reason. Insurgents in the making like Don Joaquín Valtierra y Portales (proprietor of El Coecillo), Ambrosio Montero de Espinosa (a priest known as Father Chocolate), and Father Miguel Hidalgo y Costilla himself were covertly plotting Mexico's future. Napoleon had just invaded Spain, and his brother Joseph Bonaparte had replaced King Charles IV. Spain's colonies in the Americas were in limbo. If my ancestors arrived even earlier, they also witnessed Don José Iturrigaray visit Don Joaquín Valtierra at El Coecillo in 1803. The viceroy, the king's highest representative in New Spain, had come from Mexico City to admire Guanajuato's mines in person.

Don Joaquín, the viceroy, and the others shared high political ideals. They also knew each other and had ties to Silao. Don Joaquín and Don José Iturrigaray were old friends. Father Miguel Hidalgo, who was the head priest at San Felipe and then Dolores, had family in Silao. His brother Don Manuel Mariano Hidalgo lived there with his wife, María Gertrudis Armendáriz, a native of Silao. He was also friends with El Padre Chocolate, whom he visited at the church of Señor de la Santa Veracruz in Silao.

Nevertheless, Spanish loyalists in Mexico City discovered and thwarted plans for an insurgency in September of 1808. As a result, Spanish authorities retaliated against the conspirators. Don José Iturrigaray resigned as viceroy and went to prison in Spain. Many of his supporters in Mexico City and elsewhere also paid dearly, some with their lives. In Silao, El Padre Chocolate and other co-conspirators were arrested and jailed in Guanajuato. Luisa Hernández's parents must have experienced firsthand the fear and uncertainty that gripped Silao. After all, they got married there on May 7, 1809.

My ancestors also lived through Miguel Hidalgo y Costilla's insurrection of 1810 or War of Independence (1810-1821). Consequently, they witnessed its horrors and the aftermath it left in its wake. Some examples follow. In December 1810, Spanish officials published in Silao an ordinance calling for the death of any four citizens for every royalist soldier killed. There is little doubt that suspicion and fear reigned in Silao or that innocent people died in retaliation. Also, on October 13, 1811, Imperial forces paraded the severed heads of Father Hidalgo and other leading insurgents through the streets of Silao as a sign of victory over the emancipators. They were taking them to Guanajuato, where they publically exhibited them until 1821. Finally, Spanish authorities arrested and subsequently murdered María Gertrudis Armendáriz in Mexico City in 1815. Besides being Father Hidalgo's sister-in-law, she was a devoted advocate of the fight for independence.

My ancestors likely witnessed other cruelties because some probably participated in the War of Independence. After his famous *grito* at Dolores (cry for independence), Father Hidalgo marched through the state of Guanajuato, where leagues of supporters joined his ranks. The inhabitants of Silao were not the exception. By the time Hidalgo's forces took over the city of Guanajuato on September 28, 1810, the number of professional soldiers, ranchers, and peasants (*campesinos*) bearing rifles, but mostly machetes and farming implements had reached thousands. Some had come from nearby Silao after insurgents like Ambrosio Montero de Espinosa (Padre Chocolate) recruited them at El Coecillo and other rural communities.

Circumstantial evidence suggests that Nicolás' relatives fought in the war. Pedro Gómez's premature death is an example. When his son Guillermo Gómez got married in 1827, only his mother, Josefa González, was alive. The same goes for Nicolás' parents, who were deceased when he married Luisa Hernández in 1825. Even if this were not the case, it is hard to believe that no one in the family participated in a war that raged in their backyard.

Nicolás González and Luisa Hernández lived as late as 1859. Although they remained at El Coecillo, their sons Plácido, Pedro, and Domingo moved next door to San Agustín and La Laborcita.

Lucas González was born in 1859. If Nicolás lived beyond that year, then three generations of Gonzálezes (Nicolás, Plácido, and Lucas) coexisted (see Appendix I).

Gregoria Velásquez's parents, **Mónico Velásquez** and **Eduvige Zepeda**, joined in matrimony in Marfil, in 1814 (see Map of Guanajuato). They were residents of Hacienda del Chapín in Guanajuato's district. They must have been very young because Mónico was born in 1798.

Having lived through the War of Independence (1810-1821), Mónico and Eduvige most likely experienced the same horrors and perils as my relatives in Silao.

Gregoria Velásquez's marriage to Plácido González in 1854 suggests that Mónico and Eduvige moved their family to Silao sometime after their daughter's birth. Gregoria was born in Hacienda del Chapín in 1837.

Today, San José del Chapín and San Nicolás del Chapín are two communities east of Lake La Purísima in the southern part of Guanajuato's jurisdiction. Either one, or both for that matter, could have been part of Hacienda del Chapín in the past. The fact that they are north of Irapuato's municipality (where Mónico Velásquez was born) seems to support this.

Andrés González's Paternal
Second Great-Grandparents

1.

N*icolás González* was born in León on December 6, 1799. His parents were **Juan Andrés González** and **Petra Juárez** (see Appendix II).

Juan and Petra wed in the parish church in León, on May 17, 1778. At the time, Juan was a resident of San Judas (see Map of Guanajuato). Petra was from El Pueblo del Coecillo. Today, San Judas is a small rural community in the most southern part of León's jurisdiction. El Pueblo del Coecillo (previously Cuisillo) has a well-documented history. Its origins date back to León's founding in 1576. Located across a river from León proper (today El Río de Los Gómez), it remained a separate settlement until the 1800s. As León grew into Guanajuato's largest city, it absorbed the haciendas and other communities on its fringes and turned them into *barrios* (neighborhoods). Coecillo is the oldest and most traditional.

In his book *Haciendas y Ranchos del Bajío: León 1700-1860*, David A. Brading described many of the places in León's jurisdiction associated with the Gonzálezes in this study. The statistics and descriptions he included will help the reader get a sense of what life was like in these rural communities.

According to Brading, Antonio de Obregón y Alcocer purchased San Judas and four other properties in 1783 to form the greater San Pedro del Monte (see Map of Guanajuato). De Obregón was part of a wave of miners that became *terratenientes* (landholders) in León's district starting in 1780. However, De Obregón was no ordinary miner; he was none other than El Conde de La Valenciana. King Charles III bestowed the prestigious title upon him after he discovered La Valenciana in 1767/68 – at the time the richest silver mine in Guanajuato.

By the time Juan and Petra's children were born or got married, the family lived on Hacienda El Palote (see Appendix XVI). Today the former hacienda lies submerged in the waters of Presa El Palote, which was constructed in 1954 to control León's flooding problems. Although the hacienda originated in the 1600s, part of a building that still stands today and is discernable when the water level drops dates back to 1758. In 1993, the lake became part of El Parque Metropolitano de León, Guanajuato.

Brading referenced Hacienda El Palote in his book at least 15 times. For example, in 1757, Palote had a small production in livestock. In 1758, the hacienda comprised 2,900 acres. When Cristóbal Marmolejo passed away that year, his son Francisco Cristóbal took over as the hacienda's proprietor. In 1770, the 41 workers at Palote and Palma (sister properties) were in debt with the haciendas 21 pesos. At the same time, the haciendas had not paid 12 ranch hands 208 pesos. In 1798, 20 laborers fled the hacienda, leaving behind a combined debt of about 260 pesos. In 1793, the owner of Palote paid to have his *maíz* (corn) transported to the municipality of Zacatecas. Ironically, an inventory of the hacienda from 1758 showed an adequate number of animals used to carry freight. In 1802, the *mayordomo* (overseer) at Palote earned an annual wage and had access to a piece of land within the hacienda to cultivate his corn.

When Juan and Petra's daughter Josefa González wed Pedro Gómez in 1796, she and her husband declared to be from Hacienda El Palote. They did the same when they christened their daughter María Máxima one year later. By the time their son Guillermo, who married in Silao in 1827, was born in 1799, the family lived in Lagunillas. Hacienda Lagunillas was west of Palote, close to the border between Guanajuato and Jalisco. According to Brading, Lagunillas' owners built a lake on the estate before 1755. In 1784, Antonio de Obregón y Alcocer (El Conde de La Valenciana) acquired the hacienda. The property included some 6,400 acres. The present-day community of Lagunillas might be a remnant of the former hacienda.

Nicolás González was born in Hacienda El Palote in 1799. Like his cousin Guillermo, he married in Silao twenty-some years later. It is still unknown whether Juan González and Petra Juárez died in León or Silao.

Luisa Hernández was the daughter of **Mariano Hernández** and **Felipa Anguiano** (see Appendix III). Mariano and Felipa wed in the parish church in Silao, on May 7, 1809. According to their marriage document, they were both residents of Silao. That was also the case when they christened their son José Ramón in 1814.

Felipa and Isidoro Anguiano were Domingo González's baptismal sponsors in 1831. Isidoro must have been Felipa's son or brother. Domingo was Nicolás and Luisa's child.

2.

Mónico Velásquez was born to **Francisco Velásquez** and **Juana María Bonilla** in Hacienda San Roque in Irapuato's jurisdiction (see Appendix IV).

Francisco and Juana María wed in Marfil on May 1, 1795. Francisco was from Irapuato's district but had been residing at Hacienda de Cuevas for 10 years. Juana María was a native of Cuevas.

Former Hacienda de Cuevas (originally Hacienda de Santa Catarina de las Cuevas) is south of Guanajuato and Marfil (see Map of Guanajuato).

Mónico's birth in Irapuato in 1798 shows how his family settled in his father's place of origin.

Eduvige Zepeda was the daughter of **Francisca Pérez** (see Appendix V). Eduvige used the surnames "Pérez" and "Zepeda" interchangeably. "Zepeda" might have been her father's last name. In one document she appeared as Eduvige Peguero. Based on Eduvige's marriage record, Francisca Pérez was from Hacienda del Chapín, apparently located southeast of Cuevas.

Andrés González's Paternal
Third Great-Grandparents

1.

Juan Andrés González was born in León to **Antonio Neri González** and **Susana Urquieta** (see Appendix II). According to his age in 1778, he was born in 1756. The surname "Urquieta" appeared on other records I studied. In 1799, María Luisa Urquieta was Nicolás González's baptismal sponsor.

Antonio Neri González and Susana Urquieta wed in the parish church in León, on February 17, 1754. They were both from Hacienda Santa Rosa (see Appendix XVI). Today, most people remember the former hacienda for the Polish refugees (mainly orphans) it sheltered during World War II. However, in a more distant past, it was a thriving field estate (see Map of Guanajuato). According to David A. Brading, Santa Rosa represented the type of hacienda that developed from landowners agglomerating adjoining properties. Also, Santa Rosa was an example of how some landholders rented parts of their estates to private ranchers known as *arrendatarios* (lessees). In 1733, 13 tenant farmers or lessees occupied different sections of Santa Rosa by paying the proprietor rent.

By the time Antonio and Susana christened their first child on December 3, 1754, their place of residence was El Monte. It does not come as a surprise because El Monte was most likely Susana's birthplace. Brading indicates that El Monte (also known as Tepetates) was an extension of barren land southeast of León. It

49

remained unoccupied until the local government finally distributed it among solicitors in the late 1600s.

Petra Juárez was the daughter of **Bartola de los Dolores**. Based on Petra's marriage document of 1778, Bartola was from El Pueblo del Coecillo (see the previous section). In 1825, Petra's last name appeared as "Rocha" on Nicolás González's marriage record. It might have been her father's surname.

2.

Francisco Velásquez (of Irapuato) was the son of **Jorge Alejandro Velásquez** and **Teresa Cabrera** (see Appendix IV).

Juana María Bonilla (of Cuevas) was the daughter of **Antonio Bonilla** and **Perfecta Calderón**.

Andrés González's Paternal
Fourth Great-Grandparents

1.

*A*ntonio *Neri González* was born to **Valerio González** and **Francisca Rodríguez** about 1732 (see Appendix II). In 1734, Valerio and Francisca lived on Hacienda de Sánchez in León's jurisdiction (see Appendix XVI). David A. Brading does not specify a Hacienda de Sánchez in his book *Haciendas y Ranchos del Bajío*, but he does mention a Sánchez family that prospered in landholding. Pedro Sánchez purchased 980 acres between 1750 and 1790. It is likely that his family owned properties before 1750. In 1795, his son Lorenzo Sánchez acquired the Labor de Patiña (the Patiña Field), which was between El Palote and Lagunillas (see Map of Guanajuato).

Valerio González, born about 1709, is my earliest known direct paternal ancestor (see Appendix XVII).

Susana Urquieta was the daughter of **Juan Urquieta** and **Juana Antonia Flores**. Juan and Juana Antonia resided in El Monte in León's district when they christened two of their daughters in 1729 and 1732, respectively. That explains Antonio González and Susana Urquieta's presence at El Monte in 1754 (see Appendix XVII).

Brading adds that Francisco de la Fuente, an immigrant from Santander, Spain, bought 682 acres in El Monte in 1728. He also purchased neighboring properties during the following years. Given that he owned mules and other work animals in 1730, it is likely that his business was in the transportation of goods.

Matías Urquieta was a mestizo who purchased Rancho Santa Lucía in the area of El Monte. At the time of his death in 1747, he owned oxen, mules, sheep, cattle, and mares.

Andrés González's Maternal Grandparents

*M*aría de Jesús Reyes was the daughter of **Gregorio Reyes** and **Anastacia Oliva** (see Appendix I). Gregorio was 42 years old when he passed away in 1862. Therefore, he was born in 1820. Anastacia was 36. That makes her birth year 1826.

According to his death document, Gregorio died of dysentery. He was a *jornalero* (day laborer) and resided on San José Street in Silao.

When Gregorio and Anastacia christened their son José de los Santos de Jesús in 1849, they lived in El Tecolote. This community was probably somewhere between Silao and Romita. The couple's other children included Candelario and María Refugio (Cuquita). My aunt Guadalupe Montes first heard of Cuquita from a family friend called Chonita (see Appendix XII).

Candelario Reyes and Dominga Cisneros' marriage document of January 20, 1887, confirms the existence of María de Jesús' siblings. It shows María Refugio and Valentín Cuéllar as sponsors of the wedding. It is unknown if they were a couple.

In 2000, I visited Silao's main cemetery (Panteón Antiguo), hoping to find additional information on my grandfather's maternal side. I remember the impressive walls and the entrance with its massive gate surrounding the cemetery. I also recall the mausoleums, crypts, and tombs I photographed as I searched for my ancestors' graves. I was seeking to expand my research, but I also wanted to pay my respects. Unfortunately, despite my efforts, I found nothing related to them.

As I walked back to the entrance and prepared to leave, I met the administrator of the cemetery, Mr. David Ramos, and his secretary. They searched for my ancestors in their database but came out empty handed. Apparently, if people do not claim their loved ones' burial sites by paying a fee, cemetery officials reuse them. Despite the outcome, my experience at the Panteón del Pueblo was still a great one. Knowing that I was walking in the presence of my long-gone relatives like María de Jesús Reyes and her predecessors made my time there worthwhile.

Tomasa Díaz's Parents

Eulogio Díaz and **Teresa Silva** wed in the parish church in Marfil, on November 29, 1889. Eulogio was 18 years old. Teresa was 20 (see Appendix VI).

Eulogio and Teresa were born in El Capulín and Cañada de Bustos, respectively (see Map of Guanajuato). The two communities are connected by a winding dirt road that leads to the highway to Silao on one end and to a paved road going to Marfil and Guanajuato on the other.

As newlyweds, they settled in Rancho Nuevo near Cañada de Bustos. Rancho Nuevo had been the home of the Silva family for generations. In 1992, my uncle Ignacio Caudillo showed me a small hill north of Cañada, where Rancho Nuevo had once existed (see Appendix XIII).

Eulogio and Teresa's children were my grandmother Tomasa and her sisters, Porfiria and Marcelina. The family was on the verge of growing, but sadly Teresa died in childbirth. Isidro Díaz (my grandmother's cousin) told me that she was most likely buried in El Zangarro, a community with a cemetery east of Cañada that was submerged by Lake La Purísima. Several years after I met Isidro in 1992, I discovered references to El Camposanto el Zangarro (Zangarro Cemetery) on church burial records. I also located Lake La Purísima east of Cañada de Bustos and El Capulín on maps of Guanajuato.

Eulogio Díaz remarried and had at least one daughter with his new bride. He died in Los Infantes (in Silao's district). His daughter, María Díaz, lived in Irapuato.

Tomasa Díaz's Paternal Grandparents

ulogio Díaz's parents, **Victoriano Díaz** and **Petra Saldaña,** wed in the parish church in Marfil, on November 25, 1858 (see Appendix VI).

Victoriano was born in Cañada de Bustos in 1833. He was the illegitimate son of Mauricia Díaz. His baptismal sponsors were his future wife's grandparents, Salvador Saldaña and Josefa (Inés) López (see Appendices VI & VII). Petra was born on June 27, 1840.

In 1850, Victoriano married his first wife, Senona Aguilar. They were 17 and 16 years old, respectively. She died in childbirth in 1856.

When Eulogio's sister Albina Díaz married Francisco Hernández in 1890, Victoriano and Petra were still alive. When his brother Desiderio Díaz married Gregoria in 1903, Victoriano had already passed away.

In 1992, Isidro Díaz revealed he knew his grandmother's name was Petra. I am not sure if he met her, but given his age at the time, I would think he did.

Tomasa Díaz's Paternal
Great-Grandparents

1.

*V*ictoriano *Díaz's* mother, **Mauricia Díaz**, was likely from the city of Guanajuato (see Appendix VI). There is evidence of this in the pages ahead. Also, she probably had a second son named Cosme Damián.

As mentioned in the previous section, Mauricia had a connection with the Saldaña family before Victoriano married Petra Saldaña in 1858.

2.

Petra Saldaña's parents, **Ricardo Saldaña** and **Carmen Salinas**, wed in the parish church in Marfil, on August 11, 1839 (see Appendix VI). There were other marriages between the two families.

Ricardo arrived in Cañada de Bustos with his parents and some of his siblings after his brother Modesto was born in 1830 (see Appendix XVIII). The family had left their home in La Trinidad in Dolores' jurisdiction. By this time, Ricardo's sisters Lina and Leandra Saldaña had lived in Cañada for several years.

Lina and Leandra were adolescents when they married their respective husbands in 1823 and 1824. Cesario and Antonio Díaz and their wives were the weddings' sponsors. They were residents of Guanajuato and possibly Mauricia Díaz's relatives.

In 1833, Ricardo's brother Francisco Saldaña married Ambrosia Díaz. She was the daughter of José María Díaz of Guanajuato, another potential relative of Mauricia Díaz. That same year Ricardo's parents served as Victoriano Díaz's baptismal sponsors.

Carmen Salinas was from Cuevas, which is not too far from Cañada (see Map of Guanajuato). She died on April 2, 1855 at age 30 and was laid to rest in the San Juan de Dios Cemetery, which predated El Zangarro. She must have died in childbirth because her son Francisco expired on August 5, 1855, at four months old. He was a resident of El Capulín according to his burial record. Ricardo was still alive.

Tomasa Díaz's Paternal Second Great-Grandparents

icardo Saldaña's parents, **Salvador Saldaña** and **Josefa (Inés) López**, started a family in Cruz de Piedra in Dolores' district as early as 1802 (see Appendix VII). Cruz de Piedra is located close to where the jurisdictions of Dolores Hidalgo and Guanajuato meet in the Sierra de Santa Rosa (see Map of Guanajuato).

In Dolores, the Saldaña-López family witnessed the start of Mexico's fight for independence. As residents of Dolores' municipality and as parishioners of its church, they came face to face with Miguel Hidalgo y Costilla and his brother José Joaquín. Several parish records of Nuestra Señora de los Dolores show their encounter.

Salvador and Josefa's daughter Ana Cirila de la Luz was christened on July 16, 1802. Clergymen José Ramón Vallejo and DON JOSE JOAQUIN HIDALGO Y COSTILLA signed her baptismal entry. Don José Joaquín Hidalgo died later that year. His brother Miguel, who was a priest in San Felipe, Guanajuato, asked to be transferred to Dolores. He replaced his brother there in 1803.

Salvador and Josefa's son Mariano was baptized on July 26, 1804. José Manuel de Soria and MIGUEL HIDALGO Y COSTILLA's signatures appear on his baptismal document.

On September 16, 1810, Father Hidalgo started the War of Independence with 600 men from Dolores and his famous *grito* (call for liberty and equality).

He was eventually captured and executed in Chihuahua in 1811. He is known as El Padre de la Patria (Father of the Nation) for his ideas, bravery, and ultimate sacrifice. September 16 is recognized as Mexico's Independence Day.

Salvador and Josefa moved their family from Cruz de Piedra to La Trinidad (also in Dolores' district). They later relocated to Cañada de Bustos, where they rejoined Lina and Leandra Saldaña (see Appendix XVIII). Church documents in Marfil recorded their lives there. In 1833, Salvador and Josefa served as Victoriano Díaz's baptismal sponsors. Between 1832 and 1855, several Saldaña family members got married. Ricardo and Modesto wed Carmen and Teresa Salinas (sisters). For Modesto, Teresa represented his second marriage. Carmen and Modesto's two wives had ties to Cuevas. Hacienda de Cuevas, although in decline, apparently was still a source of employment for men and women in the area, including the Saldaña brothers.

When Modesto married Rafaela Ortega in 1850, Salvador Saldaña had already passed away. Josefa López had not.

Carmen Salinas' parents, **Mateo Salinas** and **Antonia Ortega**, wed in the parish church in Marfil, on February 17, 1817. Mateo was also known as Mateo Jaramillo (see Appendix VIII).

Although Mateo was originally from Hacienda de Santiago, and Antonia from Hacienda de Cuevas, the couple settled in Rancho La Soledad (see Map of Guanajuato). It was their home when they christened their daughter María Lucía in 1822. María Lucía's godparents were from Cuevas. Rancho La Soledad was still their home when Teresa was born in 1835 and also when she married Modesto Saldaña in 1855. Nevertheless, when Carmen Salinas wed Ricardo Saldaña in 1839, she declared to be from Cuevas. It suggests that Rancho La Soledad was close to Cuevas and that the Salinas-Ortega family felt at home in both communities.

Tomasa Díaz's Paternal Third Great-Grandparents

*M*ateo Salinas was a native of Hacienda de Santiago and the son of **Victoriano Jaramillo** and **Ana Josefa Salinas** (see Appendix VIII). It is unknown why Mateo adopted his mother's surname.

Antonia Ortega was from Hacienda de Cuevas. Her parents were **Tomás Ortega** and **Catarina Rivera** (see Appendix VIII).

Tomás and Catarina wed in Marfil on November 17, 1793. They were both from Cuevas.

Tomasa Díaz's Paternal Fourth Great-Grandparents

*T*omás Ortega was the son of **Juan Bernardino Ortega** and **María Paz** (see Appendix VIII). They were from Hacienda de Cuevas.

Catarina Rivera's parents were **Luis Beltrán Rivera** and **Juana María Sanjuanero** (see Appendix VIII). Her family was also from Hacienda de Cuevas.

Tomasa Díaz's Maternal Grandparents

*T*eresa Silva was the daughter of **Germán Silva** and **Librada Plancarte** (see Appendix VI).

Germán Silva was born in Cañada de Bustos in 1837. He married his first wife, Bonifacia Olmos, in 1859. Bonifacia died of colic in Cañada in 1862. She was 21 years old. On her burial record, Germán's name appeared with his mother's last name – Corral.

Germán's second wife, Librada Plancarte, passed away giving birth in 1888. She had lived with Germán and her children in Rancho Nuevo, a stone's throw away from Cañada.

Germán married his third wife, Manuela Caudillo, on February 22, 1898. They were 60 and 48 years old, respectively. Interestingly, his son Severiano Silva married Cresencia Caudillo on the same day. At least two more of Germán's children married into the Caudillo family. There was also Porfiria Díaz-Silva, the granddaughter Germán had raised after Teresa Silva passed away. She wed Apolonio Caudillo.

The 1930 census for Cañada de Bustos listed the families of Severiano Silva y Apolonio Caudillo on the same page. Severiano's family included himself, his wife, Cresencia, and their children Ignacio (11), Pedro (8), and Cruz (6). There were also Eduviges (20) and Mariana Ortega (18). Apolonio's family consisted of himself, Porfiria, and their children Emilia (8), Catalina (6), Antolino (4), and Ignacio (2) (see Appendix XIII).

On one of my trips to Cañada, I met a member of the Silva family. My uncle Ignacio Caudillo, who introduced us, addressed the man as *tío* (uncle). Unfortunately, I forgot his name, but I would like to think he was one of Severiano's sons. In León, I met another of Germán's grandsons – Luz Silva. Luz and his wife, Aurelia Barrientos, were none other than my uncle Fernando Silva's parents (see Appendix XI).

As I dove deeper into my family history in the 1990s, I remembered my grandmother saying that my uncle Fernando Silva and aunt Fernanda González of Nuevo Laredo (a couple since the early 1950s) were cousins of sorts. One day, as I studied Germán Silva's tree, I decided to check out their kinship. Appendix XIX shows what I discovered.

Tomasa Díaz's Maternal
Great-Grandparents

ermán Silva was the son of **José María Silva** and **Juana Corral** (see Appendix VI).

José María and Juana were residents of Cañada de Bustos when they wed in Marfil on February 22, 1836. They were 22 and 18 years old, respectively.

José María's last name appeared as "Blancarte," not "Silva," on Germán's baptismal document of 1837.

José María died of dysentery in Rancho Nuevo in 1874. He was 60 years old. According to his age in 1836 and 1874, he was born in 1814.

Juana was born in Peña Caída in Marfil's jurisdiction, on June 24, 1817.

Tomasa Díaz's Maternal Second Great-Grandparents

José María Silva was the son of **María Santos Silva** (see Appendix IX). Besides "Silva" and "Corral," José María also used the surname "Blancarte." Perhaps it was his father's last name.

My uncle Ignacio Caudillo heard his elders say that our Silva relatives had roots in Santa Cruz de Juventino Rosas (see Map of Guanajuato). The truth of the matter is that I found more Silva families in the parish records in Marfil than in Santa Cruz. In my search, I even visited the cemetery and church in Santa Cruz but could not prove anything. Perhaps the Silvas did originate in Santa Cruz. Still, there is no evidence to confirm it.

Juana Corral was the daughter of **Andrés Corral** and **Andrea Ibarra**, who wed in Marfil on December 3, 1803 (see Appendix X). Andrés was from Rancho de la Peña Caída, Andrea from Ranchito de la Piedad. Apparently, these two communities disappeared with the passing of time. Dr. Antonio Peñafiel did not mention them in his list of haciendas and ranchos (in the district of Guanajuato) for the year 1892. Pedro González only referred to Peña del Panal in 1900 (89).

Marfil or Guanajuato's expanding population most likely absorbed them and turned them into *barrios* (neighborhoods). The fact that Andrés and Andrea's wedding sponsors were from Marfil and Guanajuato, respectively, seems to support this idea. Also, today there is a sector of Marfil called Peñitas.

Tomasa Díaz's Maternal Third Great-Grandparents

*A*ndrés Corral (of Rancho de la Peña Caída) was the son of **Martín de los Reyes Corral** and **María Manuela Patlán** (see Appendix X).

Andrea Ibarra (of Ranchito de la Piedad) was the daughter of **Eusébio Albino Ibarra** and **Marcela Sebastiana Juárez**.

PART III

Photographs and Facsimiles

Mauricio González, Laredo, Texas, 1989

Narciso González, Nuevo Laredo, Tamaulipas, early 1950s

Lucas González, Silao, Guanajuato, circa 1880

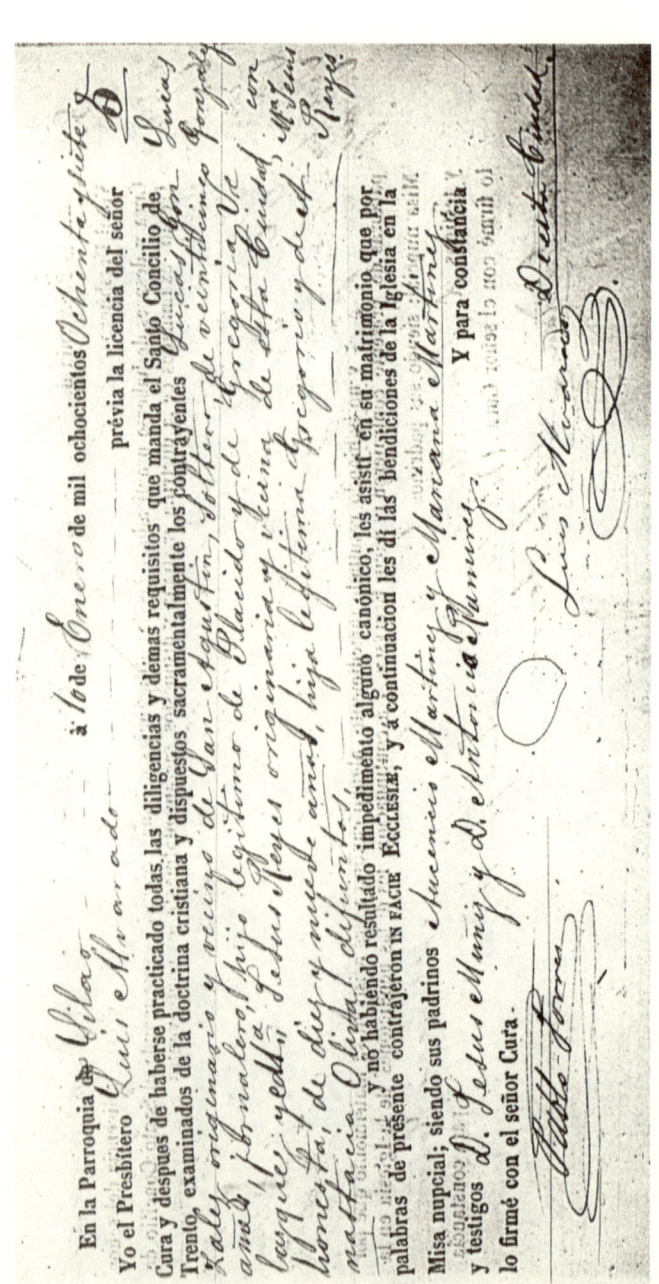

Marriage Document of Lucas González and María
de Jesús Reyes, Silao, Guanajuato, 1887

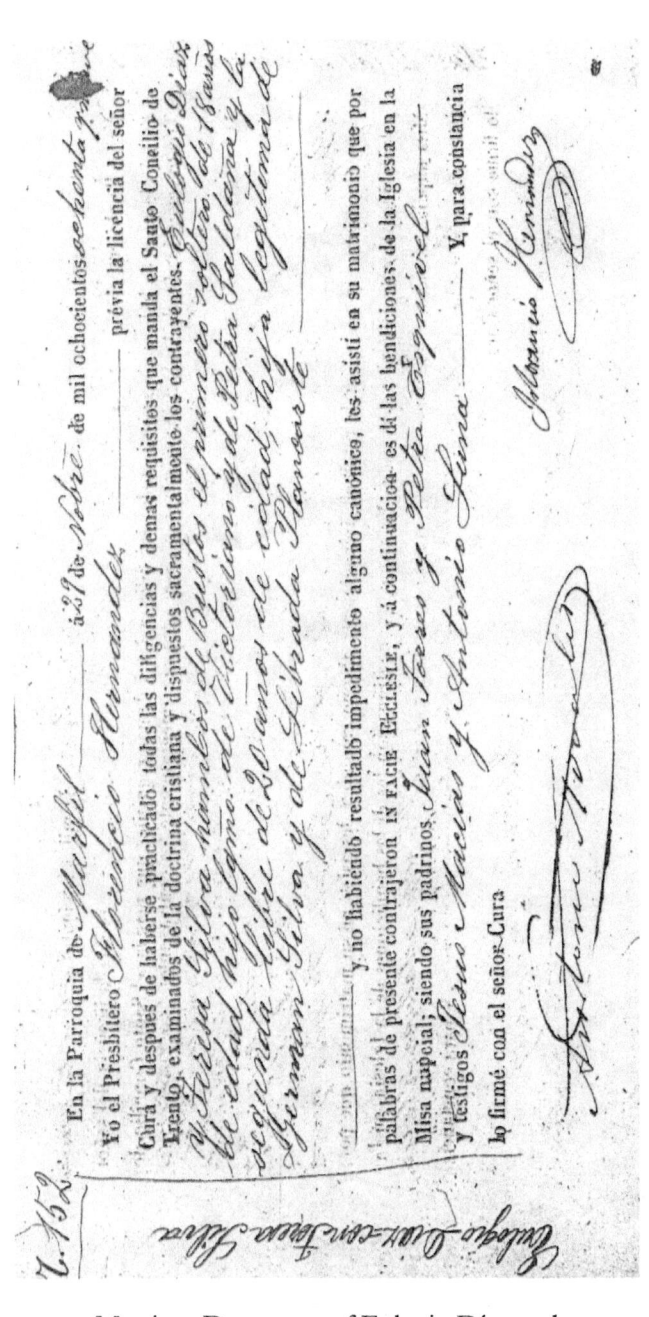

Marriage Document of Eulogio Díaz and
Teresa Silva, Marfil, Guanajuato, 1889

Baptismal Document of Nicolás González, León, Guanajuato, 1799

Left to right: Mauricio González, Guadalupe Montes, and
Juan José González II, Silao, Guanajuato, 1992

Mauricio González (right) with Luz Silva and
Aurelia Barrientos, León, Guanajuato, 1992

Mauricio (far left), Narciso, and Guillermina González with
Mr. and Mrs. Ignacio Caudillo, Cañada de Bustos, Guanajuato, 1994

Mauricio González (sporting a leather jacket from León,
Guanajuato), Hollywood, California, 1996

Mauricio González (center) with his sisters,
his aunt Guadalupe Montes, and cousins, Silao, Guanajuato, 1996

Mauricio González with Josefina Camarillo (González),
San Agustín, Guanajuato, 2002

Mauricio González with Margarito Vázquez Navarro
(Silao's historian), Silao, Guanajuato, 2002

APPENDIX I

Andrés González's Family Tree Fan Chart

APPENDIX II

Nicolás González's Family Tree Fan Chart

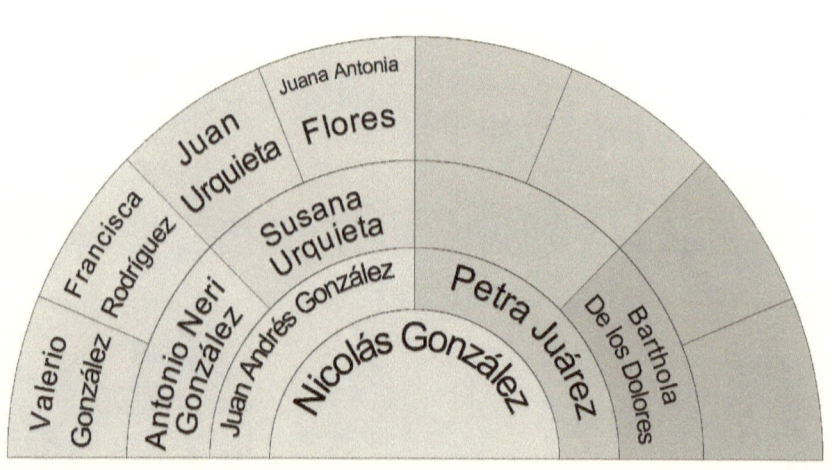

APPENDIX III

Luisa Hernández's Family Tree Fan Chart

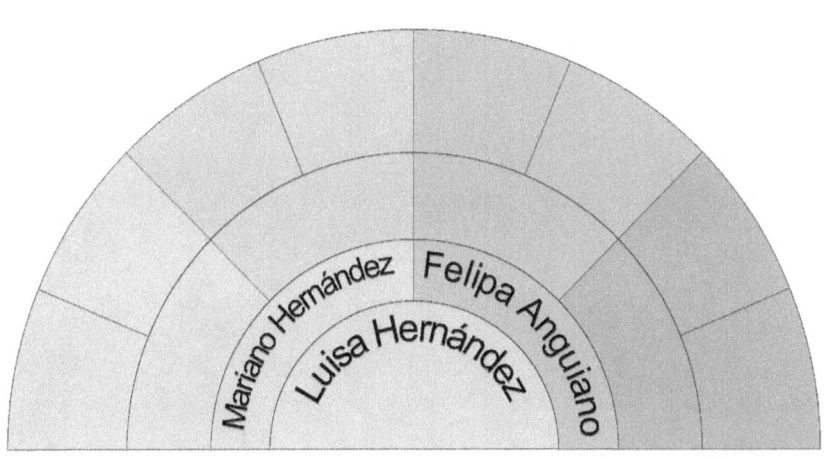

APPENDIX IV

Mónico Velásquez's Family Tree Fan Chart

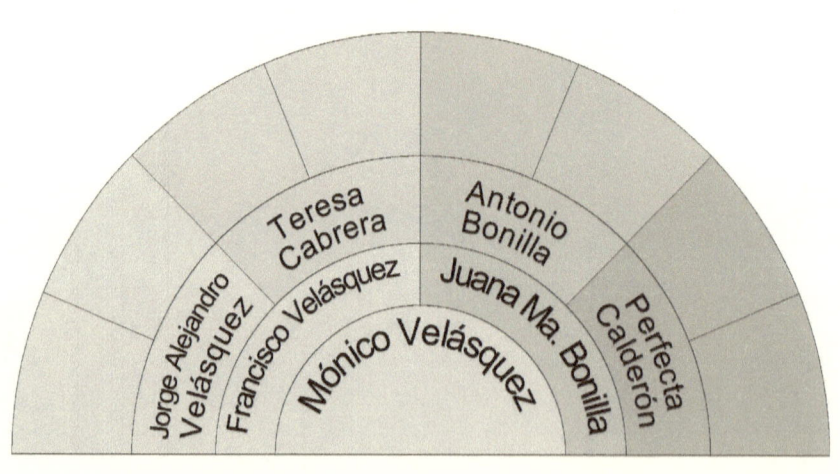

APPENDIX V

Eduvige Zepeda's Family Tree Fan Chart

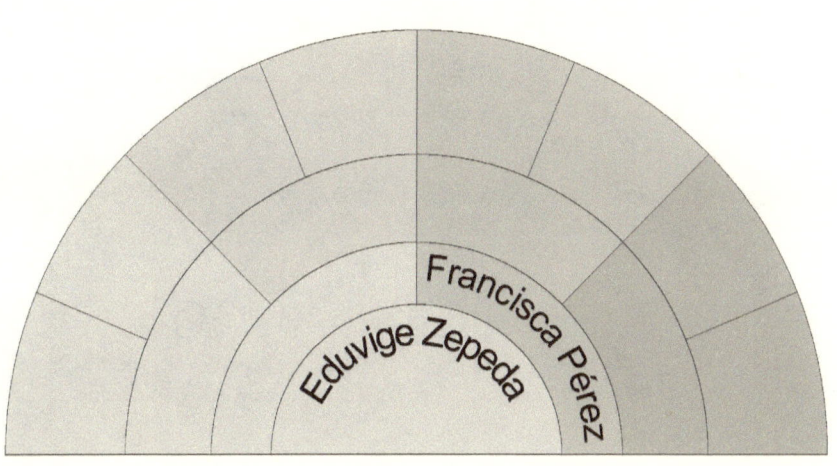

APPENDIX VI

Tomasa Díaz's Family Tree Fan Chart

APPENDIX VII

Ricardo Saldaña's Family Tree Fan Chart

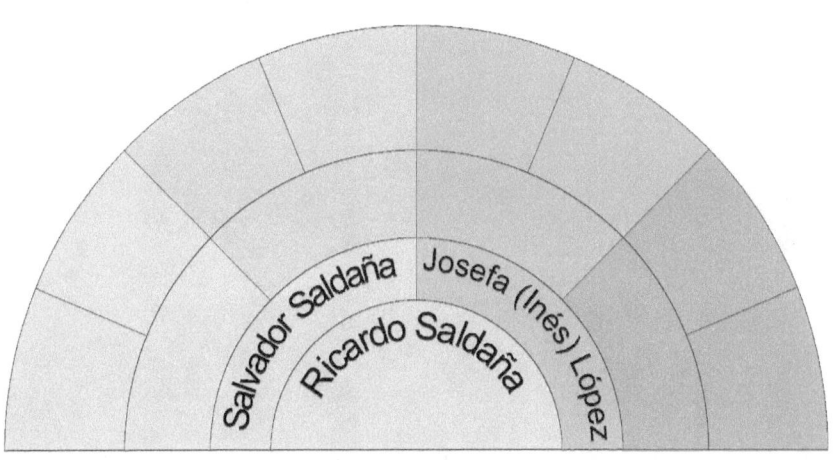

APPENDIX VIII

Carmen Salinas' Family Tree Fan Chart

APPENDIX IX

José María Silva's Family Tree Fan Chart

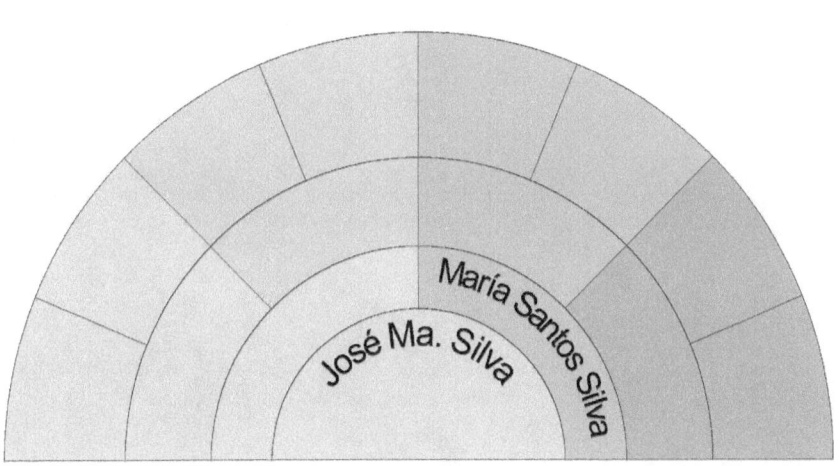

APPENDIX X

Juana Corral's Family Tree Fan Chart

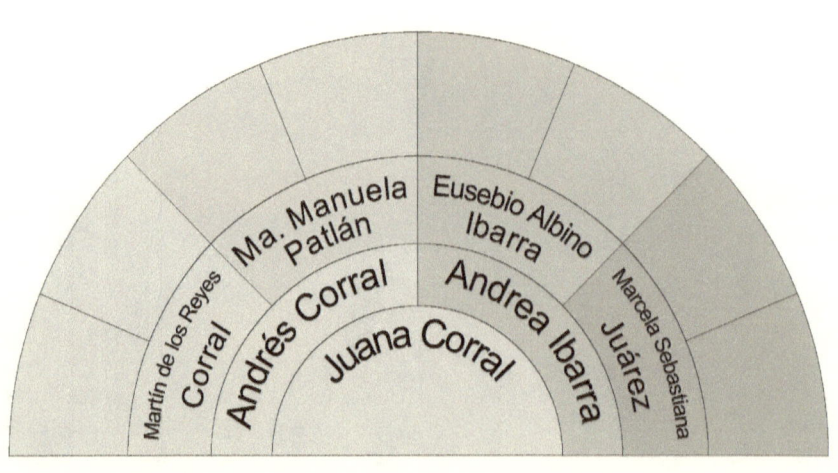

APPENDIX XI

Andrés González and Tomasa Díaz's Children and Grandchildren

Note: The following are Andrés and Tomasa's children and grandchildren who lived into adulthood.

1. María de Jesús González & Juan José González
   Ramona Mercedes
   Silvia
   Juan José II
   Víctor

2. Cándido González

3. Fernanda González & Fernando Silva
   María Guadalupe
   Mónica Irene
   José Eduardo
   María Bertha
   Benjamín
   Lilia Victoria
   Eduardo Ramón
   Julio Francisco

4. Narciso González & Noemí Raquel Rodríguez
  Gricelda Adriana
  Guillermina Araceli
  Narciso Guadalupe II
  Mauricio Javier

5. Inocencia González

APPENDIX XII

Lucas, Amado, and Preciliana González's Children and Grandchildren

Note: The following represent Lucas, Amado, and Preciliana's children and grandchildren mentioned in the book.

Lucas González & María de Jesús Reyes	Amado González & Gregoria	Preciliana González & Mucio Zúñiga

María Natividad González
  Soledad Montes
  José Natividad Montes
  Rafaela Montes
  Guadalupe Montes
  Antonio Montes
 	
Andrés González
  Florencia González
  Ma. de Jesús González
  Cándido González
  Fernanda González
  Narciso González
  Inocencia González
 	
Magdaleno González
 	
San Juana González
 	
Luz González
	Rosalío González
	  Agustín González
	  Arcadio González
	
	Micaela González
		Carmen Zúñiga
		
		María Zúñiga
		
		Aurora Zúñiga
		
		Juana Zúñiga
		
		Loreto Zúñiga
		
		Francisco Zúñiga

APPENDIX XIII

Tomasa, Porfiria, and Marcelina Díaz's Children (Mentioned in the Book)

Tomasa Díaz & Andrés González	Porfiria Díaz & Apolonio Caudillo	Marcelina Díaz & Francisco Bustos
Florencia González	Emilia Caudillo	Francisco Bustos
Ma. de Jesús González	Catalina Caudillo	Trinidad Bustos (Trino)
Cándido González	Antolino Caudillo	Eduardo Bustos (Lalo)
Fernanda González	Ignacio Caudillo (Nacho)	Joaquina Bustos
Narciso González		Trinidad Bustos (Trine)
Inocencia González		

APPENDIX XIV

Andrés González and Tomasa Díaz's Known Addresses in Silao, Guanajuato

	Addresses	Date or Time Frame	Sources
1	Arenal Street	April 26, 1930	María de Jesús Reyes' death record
2	Aurora Street	Starting May 15, 1930	Mexico's National Census of 1930
3	Aldama Street (*calle* La Luna)	1930s thru 1940s	Rafaela and Guadalupe Montes (Silao) and Josefina Camarillo (San Agustín)

APPENDIX XV

Plácido, Domingo, and Pedro González's Places of Residence during the 1850s

1	Plácido González & Gregoria Velásquez	La Laborcita San Agustín
2	Domingo González & Crisanta Juárez	San Agustín La Laborcita (de López) Labor de Aguas Buenas
3	Pedro González & Juana Hernández	San Agustín

APPENDIX XVI

The Gonzálezes in León's Jurisdiction during the 1700s

Three Generations	Year	Place of Residence
Juan Andrés González & Petra Juárez	1799 1796	Hacienda del Palote
	1778	San Judas & Pueblo del Coecillo
Antonio Neri González & Susana Urquieta	1754	Hacienda de Santa Rosa & El Monte
Valerio González & Francisca Rodríguez	1734	Hacienda de Sánchez

APPENDIX XVII

My González Lineage: 12 Generations

1	²Robert, ¹Mauricio III, ¹Sebastián, ¹Leonardo González	Laredo, Texas
2	¹Mauricio II, ²Juan, Andrés, Alberto González	Laredo, Texas
3	**Mauricio González**	Laredo, Texas
4	Narciso González	Silao – Nuevo Laredo – Laredo
5	Andrés González	Silao – Nuevo Laredo
7	Lucas González	Silao, Guanajuato
8	Plácido González	Silao, Guanajuato
9	Nicolás González	León – Silao
10	Juan Andrés González	León, Guanajuato
11	Antonio Neri González	León, Guanajuato
12	Valerio González	León, Guanajuato

APPENDIX XVIII

Saldaña and Salinas Family Members
(Mentioned in the book)

Salvador Saldaña & Josefa López	Mateo Salinas & Antonia Ortega
Ana Cirila Saldaña	
Mariano Saldaña	
Lina Saldaña	
Leandra Saldaña	
Francisco Saldaña	
Ricardo Saldaña	Carmen Salinas
Modesto Saldaña	Teresa Salinas

APPENDIX XIX

Four Generations of Silvas

1	2
Germán Silva & Bonifacia Olmos (first wife)	Germán Silva & Librada Plancarte (second wife)
Juan Silva & Soledad Luna (second wife)	Teresa Silva
Luz Silva	Tomasa Díaz
Fernando Silva	Fernanda González

Sources

Published Materials

Alvarez, Xóchitl. "Hacienda de 1758 sale a la luz tras el estiaje." *El Universal* 13 May 2012.

Arredondo, Benjamín. "Algunas de las haciendas en el estado de Guanajuato en 1900." 2012.

---. "De lo ocurrido en las haciendas del estado de Guanajuato luego de la Guerra de Independencia." 2016.

---. "Las haciendas de beneficio en Marfil, Guanajuato." 2010.

Brading, David A. *Haciendas y ranchos del Bajío: León 1700-1860.* 1986.

Garibaldi, Sara. "Haciendas de un Irapuato antiguo." *Notus* 27 July 2015.

González, Pedro. *Geografía local del estado de Guanajuato.* 1904.

Jiménez, José Alfredo. "Camino de Guanajuato" and "15 de septiembre."

Marmolejo, Lucio. *Efemérides Guanajuatenses. Tomos III (1801-1850) & IV (1851-1885).*

Means, Marjorie. "El beneficio de la plata en Santa Fe de Guanajuato durante la segunda mitad del siglo XVIII." 2012.

"Parque Felice Bonetto abre en Silao." *Gto Viaja!* 21 November 2012.

Peñafiel, Dr. Antonio. *Estadística general de la República Mexicana.* 1887.

Rionda Arreguín, Isauro. *Capítulos de historia colonial Guanajuatense.* 1997.

Rodríguez, Luis I. *Lumbre brava de mi pueblo* (Silao). 1961

Vázquez Mellado, José Arvizu. *Ensayo histórico del estado de Guanajuato.* 1971.

Vázquez Navarro, Margarito. *Silao en el tiempo colonial.* 2000.

Interviews and Conversations

Amarillo, Texas, USA
    Eduardo Bustos, 1998

Fontana, California, USA
    Víctor Montes & his mother, 1996 & 1997

Pomona, California, USA
    María & Carmen Zúñiga (telephone conversation)

Laredo, Texas, USA
    Narciso González
    Trinidad Sarmiento

León, Guanajuato, Mexico
    Luz Silva & Aurelia Barrientos, 1992

Marfil (Cañada de Bustos), Guanajuato, Mexico
    Ignacio Caudillo & wife, 1992, 1994, 1996
    Isidro Díaz, 1992

Nuevo Laredo, Tamaulipas, Mexico
    Fernando & Fernanda Silva
    Inocencia González
    Luz González
    Tomasa Díaz

Silao, Guanajuato, Mexico
    Angel Isaac Uribe, 2016 (online conversation)
    Ernestina Maldonado, 2016 (online conversation)
    Guadalupe Montes, 1992, 1996, 1997, 2000

Margarito Vázquez Navarro, 2002
Rafaela Montes, 1992 & 1996

Silao (San Agustín), Guanajuato, Mexico
Herminia González, 1996 & 2002
Josefina González (Camarillo), 1996 & 2002
Odilón Trejo, 2002

The Church of Jesus Christ of Latter-day Saints Micro-film Collection (now partly digitalized)

Dolores Hidalgo, Guanajuato, Mexico
Bautismos 1801-1804, Film number 710434
Bautismos 1818-1824, Film number 710448
Bautismos 1810-1826, Film number 710451
Bautismos 1826-1828, Film number 710452

Irapuato, Guanajuato, Mexico
Bautismos 1791-1802, Film number 632757

León, Guanajuato, Mexico
Bautismos 1717-1732, Film number 246019
Bautismos 1732-1741, Film number 246020
Bautismos 1749-1756, Film number 246022
Bautismos 1797-1800, Film number 246030

Información Matrimonial 1778, Film number 246160
Matrimonios 1722-1767, Film number 246397
Matrimonios 1767-1788, Film number 246398
Matrimonios 1788-1796, Film number 246399

Marfil, Guanajuato, Mexico

Bautismos 1815-1825, Film number 646585
Bautismos 1831-1838, Film number 646600
Bautismos 1838-1845, Film number 646601
Bautismos 1858-1869, Film number 646604
Bautismos 1864-1876, Film number 646605

Defunciones 1849-1861, Film number 646209

Matrimonios 1794-1825, Film number 646184
Matrimonios 1793-1831, Film number 646189
Matrimonios 1831-1848, Film number 646190
Matrimonios 1848-1862, Film number 646191
Matrimonios 1857-1884, Film number 646192
Matrimonios 1866-1905, Film number 646193

Marfil, Guanajuato, Mexico (Civil Records)

Defunciones 1888-1890, Film number 768673

Mexico National Census 1930, Film number 1507337

Silao, Guanajuato, Mexico (Church Records)

Bautismos 1814-1819, Film number 291881
Bautismos 1830-1831, Film number 291889
Bautismos 1848-1850, Film number 291898
Bautismos 1855-1858, Film number 291902
Bautismos 1858-1860, Film number 291903
Bautismos 1875-1877, Film number 291909
Bautismos 1880-1882, Film number 291911
Bautismos 1892-1894, Film number 291918

Información Matrimonial 1825-1826, Film number 292106
Información Matrimonial 1826-1827, Film number 292107
Matrimonios 1805-1814, Film number 291984
Matrimonios 1849-1854, Film number 291988
Matrimonios 1881-1887, Film number 291991

Silao, Guanajuato, Mexico (Civil Records)

Defunciones 1930, Film number 754680
Defunciones 1862-1866, Film number 754660

Texas, USA

Texas Deaths and Burials 1903-1973, Film number 1704026

United States Census, Caldwell County, Texas, 1940, Film number 3996

Index

Calderón, Perfecta	50, 88
Camarillo, Josefina	16, 17, 18, 82, 99
Caudillo, Antolino	27, 63, 98
Caudillo, Apolonio	27, 63, 98
Caudillo, Catalina	27, 63, 98
Caudillo, Cresencia	63
Caudillo, Emilia	27, 63, 98
Caudillo, Ignacio	20, 28, 55, 63, 66, 79, 98
Caudillo, Manuela	63
Charles III of Spain	46
Charles IV of Spain	41
"Chonita"	37, 53
Cisneros, Dominga	53
Corral, Andrés	66, 67, 94
Corral, Germán	63
Corral, Juana	65, 66, 90, 94
Corral, Martín de los Reyes	67, 94
De la Cruz, Eduardo	10
De la Fuente, Francisco	51
De los Dolores, Bartola	50, 86
Díaz, Albina	56
Díaz, Ambrosia	58
Díaz, Antonio	57
Díaz, Cesario	57
Díaz, Cosme Damián	57
Díaz, Deciderio	56
Díaz, Eulogio	27, 55, 56, 75, 90
Díaz, Isidro	20, 55, 56
Díaz, José María	58
Díaz, Marcelina	27, 28, 55, 98

González, Romana	40
González, Rosalío	16, 97
González, San Juana	37, 97
González, Sebastián	102
González, Silvia	95
González, Valerio	51, 86, 101, 102
González, Víctor	10, 95
Hernández, Francisco	56
Hernández, José Ramón	47
Hernández, Juana	39, 100
Hernández, Luisa	41, 42, 43, 47, 85, 87
Hernández, Mariano	47, 87
Hidalgo y Costilla, José Joaquín	59
Hidalgo y Costilla, Mariano	42
Hidalgo y Costilla, Miguel	41, 42, 43, 59
Ibarra, Andrea	66, 67, 94
Ibarra, Eusébio Albino	67, 94
Iturrigaray, José	41, 42
Jaime, Marina	10
Jaramillo, Mateo	60
Jaramillo, Victoriano	61, 92
Jiménez, José Alfredo	12, 13, 22
Juárez, Crisanta	39, 100
Juárez, Marcela Sebastiana	67, 94
Juárez, Petra	45, 46, 47, 50, 86, 101
López, Josefa (Inés)	56, 59, 60, 91, 103
Madero, Francisco	36
Malacara, Isabel	10
Mármol, Rafael	26, 37, 38
Marmolejo, Cristóbal	46

Marmolejo, Francisco Cristóbal	46
Martínez, Sóstenes	26
Montero de Espinosa, Ambrosio	41, 42, 43
Montes, Antonio	97
Montes, Guadalupe	15, 17, 19, 25, 26, 28, 36, 37, 38, 77, 81, 97, 99
Montes, Manuel	15, 37
Montes, José Natividad	18, 37, 97
Montes, Rafaela	15, 17, 18, 97, 99
Montes, Soledad	37, 97
Montes, Víctor M.	18
Negrete, Jorge	12, 26
Núñez, Lino	8
(de) Obregón y Alcocer, Antonio	45, 46, 47
Oliva, Anastacia	53, 85
Olmos, Ambrosio	28
Olmos, Bonifacia	63, 104
Ortega, Antonia	60, 61, 92, 103
Ortega, Juan Bernardino	62, 92
Ortega, Mariana	63
Ortega, Rafaela	60
Ortega, Tomás	61, 62, 92
Padilla, María del Socorro	18
Patlán, María Manuela	67, 94
Paz, María	62, 92
Peguero, Eduvige	48
Pérez, Francisca	48, 89
Plancarte, Librada	63, 90, 104
"Porfiria"	26, 28
Ramírez, Ana María	10

Silva, Benjamín	95
Silva, Cruz	63
Silva, Eduardo Ramón	95
Silva, Eduviges	63
Silva, Fernando	9, 19, 64, 95, 104
Silva, Germán	27, 63, 64, 65, 90, 104
Silva, Ignacio	63
Silva, José Eduardo	95
Silva, José María	65, 66, 90, 93
Silva, Juan	104
Silva, Julio Francisco	95
Silva, Lilia Victoria	95
Silva, Luz	22, 64, 78, 104
Silva, María Bertha	95
Silva, María Guadalupe	95
Silva, María Santos	66, 93
Silva, Mónica Irene	95
Silva, Pedro	63
Silva, Severiano	63, 64
Silva, Teresa	27, 55, 63, 75, 90, 104
(de) Soria, José Manuel	59
Trejo, Odilón	16
Urquieta, Juan	51, 86
Urquieta, María Luisa	49
Urquieta, Matías	52
Urquieta, Susana	49, 51, 86, 101
Vallejo, José Ramón	59
Valtierra y Portales	41, 42
Vargas, Pedro	12
Vázquez Navarro, Margarito	15, 26, 83

Velásquez, Francisco	47, 50, 88
Velásquez, Gregoria	39, 40, 43, 44, 100
Velásquez, Jorge Alejandro	50, 88
Velásquez, Mónico	43, 44, 47, 85, 88
Venegas, Refugio	28
Villa, Pancho	36
Zapata, Emiliano	36
Zepeda, Eduvige	43, 44, 48, 85, 89
Zúñiga, Aurora	18, 97
Zúñiga, Carmen	18, 97
Zúñiga, Francisco	18, 97
Zúñiga, Juana	18, 97
Zúñiga, Loreto	97
Zúñiga, María	18, 97
Zúñiga, Mucio	17, 97
(Zúñiga), Rebeca	18

www.ingramcontent.com/pod-product-compliance
Lightning Source LLC
Chambersburg PA
CBHW020534290526
45786CB00002B/865